V. T. THAYER

Religion

IN PUBLIC EDUCATION

New York

THE VIKING PRESS

1947

Printed in U.S.A. by Vail-Ballou Press, Inc.

TABLE OF CONTENTS

IN SEPTEMBER of 1875 President Ulysses S. Grant journeyed from Washington, D.C., to Des Moines, Iowa, in order to address the Army of the Tennessee. It was the year prior to the celebration of one hundred years of American independence. Naturally Grant's thoughts, like those of his former comrades in arms, dwelt upon the two wars for freedom that had made this nation possible and upon the institutions which a free people had come to prize as essential for its continued development.

It is therefore significant that Grant selected for special emphasis in his address the American public school. These are his words:

"Let us then begin by guarding against every enemy threatening this perpetuity of free republican institutions. . . . The free school is the promoter of that intelligence which is to preserve us. . . . If we are to have another contest in the near future of our national existence I predict that the dividing line will not be Mason and Dixon's but between patriotism and intelligence on the one side and superstition, ambition and ignorance on the other. . . . Let us all labor to add all needful guarantees for the security of free thought, free speech, a free press, pure morals, unfettered religious sentiments, and of equal rights and privileges to all men, irrespective of nationality, color, or religion. Encourage free schools and resolve that not one dollar appropriated for their support shall be appropriated to the support of any sectarian schools. Resolve that either the state or the nation, or both combined, shall support institutions of learning sufficient to afford to every child growing up in the land the opportunity of a good common school education, unmixed with sectarian, pagan, or atheistical dogmas. Leave the matter of religion to the family circle, the church, and the private school supported entirely by private contributions. Keep the church and state forever separate." [1]

What explains Grant's preoccupation at this time with the school?

In the first place the public school was coming of age. For some years following the adoption of the Federal Constitution there were no public schools in this country. All education was private and parochial. At the beginning of the nineteenth century, however, public schools, supported by public funds, came into existence. In the East it required some time for public education to free itself from the tainted atmosphere of the charity school. In the West, however, where competition with private education was for all practical purposes nonexistent and the proceeds from the sale of public lands were from the beginning set aside for the support of public education, the public school thrived in an atmosphere of freedom.

Nor did the public school in the West face the necessity of emancipating itself from sectarian domination. Naturally, since education was local in its control and pro-

[1] Quoted from *About the Church as Education,* by Conrad H. Moehlmann, Hinds, Hayden and Eldridge, Inc., New York, 1946, pp. 8–9.

vincial in its outlook, the school reflected the thought of
the community. But here too in the West the spirit of
tolerance for religious differences, which had evolved
slowly in the eastern states, encountered little serious
resistance. Consequently the constitutions of the western
states, as they sought admission to the Union, followed
pretty much the pattern of the constitution of Connecticut of 1818. This laid down the basic principle that school
funds "shall be inviolably appropriated to the support
and encouragement of the public, or common, schools,
throughout the State . . . and no law shall be made,
authorizing said fund to be diverted to any other use than
the encouragement or support of public or common
schools."

In harmony with this policy as well as with the growing
spirit of tolerance in religious matters, the states either
by constitutional provision or legislative enactment came
to exclude sectarian instruction from public schools.
Religious instruction, if given, must be nonsectarian.

But what constituted nonsectarian instruction soon demanded serious consideration. For a short time only, in a
country predominantly Protestant, nonsectarian teaching was interpreted to be instruction in harmony with
the religious views common to Protestants. With an increase in our Catholic population and with the steady
addition of other faiths as well, this formula became increasingly unsatisfactory; and gradually liberal-minded
Americans, who were neither Catholics nor Jews, nor
members of sects discriminated against, came to see that
the omission of religious instruction from the schools was
the only sound and feasible assurance for the rights of

children of minorities. Thus the secular school came into being.

This was the solution that President Grant endorsed in 1875. "Keep the church and state forever separate," encourage free schools, secular schools, and the outcome of a conflict "between patriotism and intelligence on the one side and superstition, ambition, and ignorance on the other," he thought, was foreordained.

To render this solution doubly certain, James G. Blaine introduced in Congress in 1876 an amendment to the Constitution embodying Grant's suggestions. This amendment passed the House of Representatives easily and failed by a few votes only of receiving the necessary two-thirds majority in the Senate. Nevertheless, individual states incorporated similar provisions in their constitutions; and while in a few states sectarian rites, such as the reading of the Bible, remained legal, by 1913 in two states only was Bible-reading mandatory, and in the country as a whole the secular school seemed firmly established. Prior to 1918 and World War I, few Americans would have predicted that religion and religious education would ever again become matters of general concern in the United States.

Today it is precisely this that has happened. Recently the American Civil Liberties Union addressed a questionnaire to state departments of education in the forty-eight states. In this questionnaire two questions relating to religious education were asked. The first inquired, "Are classes in religious instruction permitted in any school building in your state?" The second, "Is the system of released time for providing religious education outside

the school building in effect in your state?" While the re-
plies to these questions involved certain qualifications,
nevertheless, of the forty-two states answering the questionnaire, fifteen replied "yes" to the first question and
twenty-seven in the affirmative to the second.

This right-about-face with respect to the status of religion in public education is a matter of grave moment.
It can have serious consequences regarding the way in
which a people that is diverse in race, religion, and
national background decides to resolve domestic problems of living; and it has a crucial bearing upon the
spirit that is to pervade the people's relations with other
peoples in a world which, despite its many cultures, is
daily becoming more closely interknit.

To portray briefly the rise of the American secular
school and to consider the full import of the challenge
now directed against it, is the purpose of this book.

Chapter I

IN THE past two hundred years the American people have evolved a unique institution expressive of the best in American life. This institution is the American public school. It is a free school, providing education at public expense for all young people within a specified age range. It is a free institution also in that it assists young people of varied abilities and diverse backgrounds to develop their talents and to realize their best possibilities. It is a democratic institution, being responsive to the character of the community it serves and being largely controlled by the local community. Finally, it is a secular school, having discovered ways in which ideals common to the American way of life can be taught without affiliation with specific religious organizations.

This is not to say that the public school is "godless," as some charge. It respects the religious convictions and the sincere doubts alike of all who entrust their children to its care. Here, too, it is unique. In the course of its history it has discovered that the ideals and values which Americans hold dear do not require a sectarian label or an arbitrary religious grounding. Its teachers have learned how to inspire a religious devotion to democratic

1

ideals—a respect for the worth and integrity of human beings, an uncommon faith in the potentialities of the common man, a conviction that people realize their best selves in the process of serving others—without the necessity of grounding these ideals arbitrarily in any one religious philosophy. This is hardly identical with religion!

To attain this rare combination of religious neutrality on the one hand and positive education in the ideals of American democracy on the other has been a long and slow process. It marks the evolution of the school from a sectarian institution with narrow, religious interests into the nonsectarian school,[1] and finally into the secular school of today.

It is difficult to exaggerate the importance of the secular school as an Americanizing agency. During the latter part of the nineteenth century and the first decades of the twentieth, people of new and strange faiths flocked to America as a haven and a refuge. Protestant and Jew, Catholic and Greek Orthodox, Russian Orthodox, Hindu, Mohammedan—in short, representatives of every conceivable faith—came to reside in the cities and towns and rural communities of the United States. Since the history of each sect holds the living tradition of a struggle for existence against a rival—a struggle in which all too often quarter was neither asked nor given—except for the secular school religious differences would have led to conflict and disorder far in excess of that which in fact

[1] See Chapter III for a discussion of this evolution. Nonsectarian instruction originated as a device for teaching what is common to a number of sects and omitting creedal points of difference. It was a happy solution in predominantly Protestant communities of mixed religious groups.

has occurred. Fortunately, the children of these immigrants of many creeds found here a school in which they learned, as Americans all, that in this country difference in religion is a right and a privilege which each can enjoy without fear of molestation. But even more significant, they learned that common ways of thinking, of acting, and of feeling toward people, and ideals of right and wrong which constitute the living tissue of sensitive and creative relationships, are the monopoly of no one religious faith. This they learned, not exclusively in the classroom or from the textbook, but from a mingling together on the playground and in extracurricular activity that reinforced the instruction of the classroom. From all these experiences there emerged ideals of fellowship which overarch differences of inheritance from foreign-born parents. Thus out of the many there came the one: the spirit of American democracy at its best.

I do not wish to imply that the secular school as described above can be found in every community of the United States. We can hardly hope for this, since schools are local institutions and reflect of necessity the cultural status of the people they serve. It is more accurate to say that I have outlined the goal toward which the American school has been moving steadily for the past century and more. In some sections of the country all that I have indicated has been achieved. In other localities atavistic conceptions and practices still persist.

For example, there are communities in Maine, near the French-Canadian line, so predominantly Catholic that the state sees nothing amiss in paying the salaries of nuns and priests and forcing the children of non-

Catholics either to attend these schools or to travel at great inconvenience to a remote school more nearly in accordance with the American pattern. On the other hand, there are schools in the Deep South of predominantly Protestant complexion, in which

"Assembly is held three times a week, opened with Bible reading and prayer, usually the Lord's Prayer is repeated in concert. For variety Bible verses are memorized and repeated in concert. Once a year the minister of each denomination is asked to speak at assembly period. Each Monday the children are asked if they attended any Sunday school or church the preceding Sunday. A record is kept." [2]

Similar deviations from the principle of separation of church and state occur in states east and west as well as north and south; but up to the present they have caused no grave concern. Rather they have been viewed as exceptions to the general rule. Usually they reflect the existence of a relatively homogeneous population; and since a high degree of control over schools resides in the local community, deviation from general practice does not startle us. "Just wait," we say, "until the population becomes more varied, and the good old American principle will assert itself."

But this policy of watchful waiting for retarded communities to catch up with democratic practices is no longer safe. Exceptions to the traditional principle of excluding sectarian religious teachings from the public schools are no longer peculiar to backward communities or to localities of predominantly one sect. Powerful forces

[2] *Information Service,* Department of Research and Education, Federal Council of the Churches of Christ in America, Vol. XIX, No. 43 (December 28, 1940).

are undermining steadily and with considerable success the principle of separation of church and state. As one investigator stated in a recent article:

"Today, in the midst of a world war to defend democratic institutions, we find thoughtful Americans in nearly every walk of life agreeing to the breakdown of that cardinal principle and accepting with little or no protest the invasion of the schools by the church. Liberal Congressmen, liberal educators and social scientists, as well as both branches of the labor movement, with few exceptions have endorsed the Mead-Aiken Federal Aid to Education bill (S.717) pending in Congress, which would allocate $300 million annually to the schools of the country, non-public as well as public, *including parochial schools of all religious denominations.*" [3]

Observe that attacks on the principle of separation of church and state operate on the national level as well as in state and locality. Nor are attempts to breach the wall directed against one point only.

They include attempts of religious groups not only to gain a foothold in the public school itself, but also to secure subsidies from the state for their own private enterprises. As evidence, observe the following trends:

1. In 1913 only two states retained mandatory provision for the reading of the Bible in the public schools. Twenty years later twelve states and the District of Columbia required its reading; in eighteen states it was optional; and in eleven only was it prohibited.

2. In states where constitution or statute now forbids religious instruction within the schools, provision is

[3] Lucile B. Milner, "Church, State and Schools," *New Republic*, CXIII (August 13, 1945), pp. 177–180.

being made increasingly to provide this instruction on a released-time program, sometimes within the school building, sometimes in church schools, but always with the assistance of the school authorities in the enrollment of children and the enforcement of attendance. Indeed, not infrequently the dismissal of children for religious instruction is carried on in defiance of a state law which public officials lack both the conviction and the courage to enforce. Probably in well over a thousand communities of the country today programs of religious education on released time are in operation.

3. Nor are violations of the traditional relationship between church and state confined to matters of instruction. In recent years religious groups have made strenuous efforts to induce both state and Federal governments to share the expenses of parochial education. In a number of states recent legislation sanctions the use of public funds for the transportation of children to private schools. In four states parochial schools receive free textbooks at public expense. Moreover, this practice has been sustained by the Supreme Court of the United States on the theory that it is the child and not the school which benefits in these instances.[4] This success seems to have breached the dike, and private interests are pressing hungrily for the further extension of grants to parochial schools—grants for health services, for the financing of needy students, for the construction of essential buildings, and for the subsidizing of teachers' salaries.

[4] 281 U.S. 370 (1930).

On the national level the friends of parochial schools have linked Federal aid to non-public schools with the obvious need for financial assistance to state school systems. Few people deny the importance of lending a helping hand to education within the states. They recognize that young people from impoverished states tend to migrate to more favorable locations, and that local handicaps in education affect adversely the welfare of the country as a whole. In education, as in the area of health and hygiene, disease and malnutrition in one locality tend to injure another. Consequently, it behooves the people of the United States to distribute evenly the advantages of education. Knowing this full well, powerful interests in Congress are saddling all legislation directed toward equalizing educational opportunities with provisions for assistance to non-public as well as to public schools.

4. Finally, the traditional alignment of Christian sects is undergoing change. The principle of separation of church and state is a Protestant, not a Catholic, doctrine. It was Protestant fear of Catholics that originally lent support to the policy of barring the state treasury against all religious groups. Catholics have always believed that, while an obligation rests upon the state to finance education, the family and the church are to exercise the actual functions of education. Today an increasing number of non-Catholic as well as Catholic voices are being raised on behalf of a plan whereby taxes paid for education are to be divided between religious and public schools. In short,

it is proposed that the state undertake to support parochial as well as public school education.

How do we explain this reversal in policy and practice, this repudiation of a policy that in the course of years has brought about a high degree of harmony and common understanding within a people once divided into highly conscious and often antagonistic religious sects? This question we shall seek to answer in chapters that follow. Let us consider first, however, the major factors that led to the separation of church and state and the evolution of the secular school. Following this brief excursion into the past we shall face directly the critical problem of the place of religion in the public school of today.

Chapter II

THE STATE SEPARATES FROM THE CHURCH

JAMES BRYCE, in his monumental work, *The American Commonwealth*, opens his chapter on "The Churches and the Clergy" with this observation:

"Half the wars of Europe, half the internal troubles that have vexed European states, from the Monophysite controversies in the Roman empire of the fifth century down to the Kulturkampf in the German empire of the nineteenth, have arisen from theological differences or from the rival claims of church and state. This whole vast chapter of debate and strife has remained virtually unopened in the United States. There is no Established Church. All religious bodies are absolutely equal before the law, and unrecognized by the law, except as voluntary associations of private citizens." [1]

Lord Bryce also remarks of the separation of church and state that "of all the differences between the Old World and the New this is perhaps the most salient."

This unique phenomenon in American life evolved slowly. Nor were there obvious indications in the Colonial period that the principles enunciated by Roger Wil-

[1] Second Edition, Revised. New York: Commonwealth Publishing Co., 1908, II, p. 643.

liams in Rhode Island as early as 1636—respect for individual conscience and separation of church and state
—would one day become the settled policy of the entire
land. On the contrary, a century of settlements seemed
to have created out of the Colonies a veritable Pandora's
box of future religious conflicts. With the exceptions of
Rhode Island, Pennsylvania, Delaware, and New Jersey,
efforts were made early in each colony to restrict the
privilege of residence to the faithful, although the nature of the true faith varied from colony to colony. In
Virginia and the South the Church of England predom-
inated. However, in the western sections of Virginia,
North Carolina, and Georgia, nonconformists—Quakers,
Baptists, Huguenots, and Presbyterians—constituted an
ever-growing aggressive and dissident group, destined
eventually to resist successfully the legal monopoly of
Episcopalianism. In New England the heavy hand of
the Puritans insured the reign of Congregationalism.
But even here an occasional Quaker, Baptist, and Presbyterian group as well as the Episcopal Church ventured to challenge the permanent control of Congregationalism.

In the Middle Colonies, fortunately, no one denomination acquired a monopoly. I say fortunately, since out
of the initial tolerance of Pennsylvania, New Jersey,
Delaware, and, in its beginnings, Maryland, the spirit of
accommodation was to spread to other colonies. The
Middle Colonies early became a melting pot of religious
groups. Here Quaker and Mennonite, Lutheran and Re-
formed German, Baptist and Methodist, Presbyterian

and Anglican, even Catholic and Jew, rubbed shoulders.
Indeed, prior to the War for Independence some sixteen
distinct Christian sects thrived. Moreover, from the western portions of these colonies there moved along the
natural river valleys "wave after wave of religious immigrants to make the British colonies into a religious crazy
quilt and Amendment I a necessity." [2]

One thing all Protestant sects possessed in common:
they hated and feared Catholicism. Maryland began as a
haven for Catholics. In 1634 Lord Baltimore established
the colony and immediately extended a friendly hand
toward other sects. But this state of good will was short-
lived, lasting scarcely more than fifty years. Under the
leadership of a retired clergyman by the name of John
Goode the people of Maryland, having been inflamed by
false reports of a conspiracy of Catholics and Indians
to massacre all Protestants, arose in revolt against the
Catholics. Needless to say, when peace was restored Roman Catholics had lost both their civil and religious
liberties. Only in Pennsylvania were Catholics permitted
from the beginning to practice their religion, whereas
in Massachusetts the hard crust of Puritanism resisted
long after the Revolution the spirit of tolerance generated in the new nation by companionship in arms and
by a common dedication to a common cause. For some
years following the adoption of the Federal Constitution, with its provision that Congress "shall make no
law respecting an establishment of religion or prohibit-

2 Conrad H. Moehlman, *School and Church: The American Way*. New
York and London: Harper and Brothers, 1944, p. 10.

ing the free exercise thereof," a Catholic priest might venture to enter the State only on penalty of life imprisonment.

Need I add that the intolerant spirit which Protestants manifested toward each other and toward Catholics was directed as well against the Jew?

For example, in 1762 two Jews in "liberty-loving" Rhode Island petitioned for naturalization. The Superior Court refused their request with an ironical interpretation of the letter rather than the spirit of the Act of 1663. The grounds given were that the "free and quiet enjoyment of the *Christian religion* and a desire of propagating the same were the principal views with which this colony was settled, and by a law made and passed in the year 1663, no person who does not profess the Christian religion can be admitted free to this colony. This court, therefore, unanimously dismiss this petition as wholly inconsistent with the principles upon which the colony was founded and a law of the same now in force." [3]

Since the Jew constituted a minority of minorities, historians have comparatively little to say of his treatment in the early days. Nevertheless, small numbers found means of slowly beating against the current. By 1775 they were present in virtually every colony.[4] Moreover Judaism, in proportion to its numbers, contributed loyally and heavily in money and men to the support of the Revolution.

Such were the conditions out of which evolved the

[3] Moehlman, *op. cit.*, p. 12.

[4] It is estimated that the Jewish population numbered less than 3,000 in 1790.

American spirit of tolerance in religion and the principle of separation of church and state. Continued strife generated eventually a spirit of live and let live, and out of war came a longing for peace.

As a matter of fact, the Colonial wars were prime factors in bringing about a spirit of mutual toleration. War with its shared experiences on battlefield and campground fostered a common fellowship. And discussions around the campfire or on the weary march stimulated the transplanting of ideas.

The orthodox foresaw in this a danger. Woodbridge Riley, in his *American Philosophy, The Early Schools,* quotes an ominous prediction which one Ezra Stiles of Newport emitted in 1759 with respect to the probable effects of the Seven Years' War. Said he:

"I imagine the American Morals & Religion were never in so much danger as from our Concern with the Europeans in the Present War. . . . I look upon it that our Officers are in danger of being corrupted with vicious principles, & many of them I doubt not will in the End of the War come home minute philosophers initiated in the polite Mysteries & vitiated morals of Deism. . . . and I make no doubt, instead of the Controversies of Orthodoxy & Heresy, we shall soon be called to the defense of the Gospel itself." [5]

Nor was Stiles a false prophet. The mingling of the Colonial militiamen with their European comrades resulted both in wearing down provincialism and in familiarizing the Colonial with the more tolerant rationalism that was becoming prevalent in Europe. As one writer

[5] Quoted by G. Adolph Koch in *Republican Religion: The American Revolution and the Cult of Reason.* New York: Henry Holt & Co., 1933, pp. 16–17.

comments, "thus the militiaman on returning from the campaign introduced his newly acquired habits of thinking and of life among the humble people of his town or wayside hamlet. Judging from the reported change in the religious tone of such a town as New Britain, no society was too secluded to escape the baneful contagion." [6]

Then, too, the acts of England afforded ample opportunity for religious sects in the colonies to rally as a unit against the common enemy. The attempts of the Bishop of London and of his sympathizers here and abroad to establish an American episcopate were opposed equally by the leaders of the Episcopal Church in America and by members of the numerous denominations who feared that their existence was thus threatened. The danger of religious control was real.[7] But equally potent was the fear that, once the Church of England succeeded in extending its control in the colonies, Parliament would eventually levy taxes for its support. These fears were confirmed locally by the general tendency of Tories of an Episcopal persuasion to support an American episcopate at precisely the time when the English government was attempting to tax the colonies "without representation" for other purposes.

[6] Richard J. Purcell, *Connecticut in Transition, 1775–1818.* For an excellent review of changes in thought and attitude in this period, see G. Adolph Koch above.

[7] "John Adams was of the opinion that New England was aroused to revolution by 'a general and just apprehension that bishops, dioceses, churches, priests and taxes were to be imposed on us. If Parliament could tax us, they could also establish the Church of England.' Jonathan Mayhew said, 'Nay, it is credibly reported that some of the warm Episcopalians have said they hoped for a time when they might shoot dissenters as freely as they might shoot pigeons.' " Moehlman, *op. cit.,* p. 38.

This common danger caused rebels in Anglican Virginia to join hands with the Congregationalists of New England. But it did more. It united the Anglican of Virginia, who favored local taxes for the support of the Episcopal Church, with his nonconformist neighbor, who opposed an established church of any variety. Temporarily the two fought shoulder to shoulder against the foreign aggressor; but obviously the principle thus held in common was a two-edged sword.

The steady growth of wealth in the colonies also tended to encourage more urbane ways of living and thinking. John Wesley once remarked that "wherever riches have increased, the essence of religion has decreased in proportion." This followed, as he saw it, from the fact that "religion must produce industry and frugality, and these cannot but produce riches. But as riches increase, so will pride, anger and love of the world in all of its branches."

Certain it is that in New England material well-being gradually shifted emphasis from conditions essential for a life of bliss in the hereafter to the refinements and enjoyments of the here and now. This in turn diminished the importance in men's eyes of creedal differences. Moreover, the production of wealth both encouraged and resulted from trade and intercourse with other people. Transactions that began with a friendly exchange of goods led easily to an exchange of ideas. Isolation in provincial America, like isolation in twentieth-century America, lessened with improved communications; and, as people communicated more freely, they also discovered common interests and a basis for mutual respect.

Wealth and easy communication likewise foster education. Peace with France in 1763 encouraged both the settlement of Frenchmen in this country and the study of the French language in schools and colleges. Americans at home as well as Americans who studied in England and France were influenced profoundly by Deism and French rationalism in philosophy and religion. In Massachusetts, Harvard College became a center from which the more tolerant and humane ideas of Deism [8] challenged traditional notions of God and of Nature; and Yale, which was founded in part to combat the "heresies" emanating from Harvard, found it increasingly difficult to identify learning and inquiry with bigotry and intolerance. As Charles and Mary Beard point out, the intellectual leaders of the Revolution constituted to a considerable extent an emancipated group. "When the crisis came," they write, "Jefferson, Paine, John Adams, Washington, Franklin, Madison and many lesser lights were to be reckoned among either the Unitarians or the Deists. It was not Cotton Mather's God to whom the authors of the Declaration of Independence appealed; it was to 'Nature's God.' From whatever source derived, the effect of both Unitarianism and Deism was to hasten the retirement of historic theology from its empire over the intellect of American leaders and to clear the atmosphere for secular interests." [9]

Deism was peculiarly fitted to offset the divisive influences in the American religious scene. Its concept of

[8] Faith in one God based more upon the study of nature and pagan literature than upon the Bible and Christian creeds.
[9] *The Rise of American Civilization.* New York: The Macmillan Co., 1930 (one volume edition), p. 449.

man and of nature was optimistic when contrasted with
the fatalism of Calvinism. It fostered the study of nature
and of science, the discovery of new truth, as against the
applications of truth salted down for all time. And it was
peculiarly adapted to the function of uniting minds of
different religious backgrounds in a common faith that
discounted the importance of creed. To the Deist the
squabbles of the theologian seemed petty indeed, and the
attempt to control the range of men's minds seemed
inimical to progress. Accordingly we find not only
Thomas Jefferson, whom his opponents falsely de-
nounced as an atheist, but the Father of His Country
as well, speaking impatiently of the monopolistic tendencies of the churches. Thus George Washington wrote
to the Catholic Bishop of Baltimore in 1790 expressing
the hope that "as mankind become more liberal, they
will be more apt to allow that all who conduct themselves
as worthy members of the community are equally entitled to the protection of civil government." On another occasion he exclaimed:

"Of all the animosities which have existed among mankind, those which are caused by difference of sentiments in
religion appear to be the most inveterate and distressing, and
ought most to be deprecated. I was in hopes, that the light-
ened and liberal policy, which has marked the present age,
would at least have reconciled Christians of every denomination so far, that we shall never again see their religious disputes carried to such a pitch as to endanger the peace of society." [10]

[10] Quoted by Charles A. Beard in *The Republic*. New York: The
Viking Press, 1943, p. 169.

And Thomas Jefferson remarks, in his *Notes on the State of Virginia:*

"Millions of innocent men, women and children, since the introduction of Christianity, have been burnt, tortured, fined, imprisoned, yet we have not advanced one inch toward uniformity. What has been the effect of coercion? To make one-half the world fools, and the other half hypocrites. To support roguery and error all over the earth. Let us reflect that it is inhabited by a thousand millions of people. That these profess probably a thousand different systems of religion. That ours is but one of that thousand. That if there be but one right, and ours that one, we should wish to see the nine hundred and ninety-nine wandering sects gathered into the fold of truth. But against such a majority we cannot effect this by force. Reason and persuasion are the only practicable instruments."

On coercion of thought, he states:

"But our rulers can have no authority over such natural rights, only as we have submitted to them. The rights of conscience we have never submitted, we could not submit. We are answerable for them to our God. The legitimate powers of government extend to such acts only as are injurious to others. But it does me no injury for my neighbor to say there are twenty gods, or no God. It neither picks my pocket nor breaks my leg. . . . Constraint may make him worse by making him a hypocrite, but it will never make him a truer man. . . . Reason and free inquiry are the only effectual agents against error."

While science and philosophy were busy freeing the minds of the intelligentsia, John Wesley and his disciples were active in democratizing the religious sentiments of the common people. Religious revivals shifted emphasis from creedal disputes and intellectual hair-splitting to salvation from sin by means of prayer and conversion. The test of a man's right to preach the Gospel was conditioned no longer upon his learning. On the contrary, he must be "called of the Lord"; and the source and sanction of right action derived more from the in-dividual's own inner conviction, his private conscience —especially in answer to prayers for guidance—than from the dictates of outer authority.

This democratic trend in religion extended beyond the denominational limits of Methodism. It was an in-tegral part of the general revolt against authority which found expression in the conflict between the Colonies and the Crown in the political sphere, and in the strug-gle of the common people against the privileges of class and tradition within the states, and against the exaction of tribute from men of all faiths for the benefit of one favored sect.

The political and religious situation in Virginia, prior to the Revolution, encouraged efforts at religious eman-cipation. Here the religious liberalism of men like Madi-son and Jefferson lent support to the democratic forces on the frontier, where Baptist and Methodist, Presby-terian and other sects opposed taxation in support of the Church of England. Virginia had courted trouble originally by welcoming settlers irrespective of their religion to the fertile country of the Blue Ridge, as buffer settlements against Indian attack. John Fiske, in *The Critical Period of American History*, states: "So long as these frontier settlers served as a much needed bulwark against the Indians, the church saw fit to ignore them and let them build meeting-houses and carry on religious services as they pleased." But once the danger was passed attempts were made both to tax them in support of the Church of England and "to compel them to receive Episcopal clergymen to preach for them, to bless them in marriage, and to bury their dead." [11]

Trouble began under dramatic circumstances when three Baptist preachers were hailed before the court in Spottsylvania and charged with "preaching the Gospel contrary to law." Patrick Henry had ridden over rough roads to attend the trial. When he heard the indictment against these men read, so reminiscent of persecutions in the past, he interrupted the Court with the question: "May it please your worship, what did I hear read? Did I hear an expression that these men whom your worships are about to try for misdemeanor, are charged with preaching the gospel of the Son of God!" [12]

In 1776 Jefferson and Madison secured the passage of a bill in Virginia which legalized all forms of worship and exempted dissenters from parish rates; and in 1785 the State took the final step in passing the Religious Freedom Act, which disestablished the Episcopal Church, abolished all parish rates, and forbade the use of religious tests for office.

Other states were not slow in taking similar action. Indeed, as the population of the states increased in diversity, these two principles of freedom of conscience and separation of church and state seemed happy guaran-

[11] Boston: Houghton Mifflin & Co., 1889, p. 80.
[12] Ibid., pp. 80–81.

tees for peace. Thus, in 1776 we find North Carolina providing in its constitution that "all men have a natural and inalienable right to worship Almighty God according to the dictates of their own consciences." Vermont, in the following year, adopted a like provision, adding, however, the importance of the Scriptures as a guide for conscience. The constitution states "that all men have a natural and inalienable right to worship Almighty God, according to the dictates of their own consciences and understanding, regulated by the word of God."

The War for Independence created a favorable situation in which to legalize principles of liberty. A number of the states were required to rewrite their constitutions in harmony with the fact of separation from England. Likewise a national government was essential in order to perpetuate the union of the Colonies and to create the machinery with which to serve common necessities. Finally the unorganized territories in the West had to be prepared for future membership in the Union.

With respect to the national government the composition of the Constitutional Convention in itself dictated tolerance of all faiths and special privilege for none. The Convention's membership included Episcopalians, Congregationalists, Presbyterians, Quakers, one Methodist, and two Catholics.[13]

The delegates agreed, in Article VI, to prohibit religious tests "as a qualification to any office or public trust under the United States." Later popular demand required the addition of the First Amendment, which prohibits an established church and guarantees freedom of

13 Moehlman, *op. cit.*, p. 43.

worship. This left each state free, however, to determine its own policies in matters of religion.

According to Charles Beard, the members of the Convention avoided as much as possible the issue of religion because of fear of stirring up sectarian controversy and thus jeopardizing the acceptance of the Constitution. "On practical grounds," he states, "the framers thought it best not to meddle with religion at all, had they been so inclined, and most of them were not so inclined." [14]

When it came to ratifying the Constitution by the states, however, representatives of all sects seized upon the religious issue, and out of concern to safeguard the states from any attempt at Federal control in religion came eventually Amendment I.

As I have said, Amendment I leaves individual states free to act as they wish on the religious issue. While most of them acted in harmony with the spirit of the Federal Constitution, not all did so promptly. For example, Connecticut and Massachusetts, with characteristic New England independence, delayed action until after the turn of the century; Connecticut until 1818 and Massachusetts until 1833.

The direction in which states newly admitted to the Union would go was foreshadowed in the Ordinance of 1787 governing the territory northwest of the Ohio River. This act insured that "no person, demeaning himself in a peaceable and orderly manner, shall ever be molested on account of his mode of worship, or religious sentiments, in the said territories." Since the Federal Constitution went into operation very shortly after

[14] *The Republic,* p. 167.

the passage of this ordinance, both religious liberty and separation of church and state were obviously assured in the territories. The example of the national government induced the states which were later carved out of western territory to incorporate in their constitutions provisions relating to religion, similar to those in the Federal Constitution.

The clear purpose of these safeguards, contrary to recent assertions, was not unfriendly to religion as such. The men responsible for them would have viewed such a suggestion with horror. Rather was it to realize within the individual states objectives similar to those of the national government. And these, as Judge Joseph Story remarked long ago, in his *Commentaries on the Constitution of the United States,* were "to cut off forever every pretense of any alliance between church and state in the national government." No one challenged the importance of religious values within the lives of individuals, but the attempt on the part of one man or a group of men to define for others the nature and the content of these values had borne thus far only sour fruit. Consequently a new policy was required, a policy of neutrality and of tolerance, of reliance upon reason and persuasion, of free communication and free thought in bringing about religious conviction: in short, education—an education in which would be permanently assured equality of opportunity for all and special privilege for none.

Nor has there been occasion until recent years to question seriously the wisdom of this action. Contrary to the fears of the established churches at the time, re-

ligious denominations thrived under the new policy.
Writing on this subject in *The American Commonwealth* a century later, James Bryce observed that "so
far from suffering from the want of State support, religion seems in the United States to stand all the firmer
because, standing alone, she is seen to stand by her own
strength. No political party, no class in the community,
has any hostility either to Christianity or to any particular Christian body. The churches are as thoroughly
popular, in the best sense of the word, as any other institutions of the country." [15]

Before we examine attempts in contemporary America
to modify this traditional policy of separation of church
and state, we shall have to trace a second step in the
emancipation of our people from sectarian control: the
freeing of education in the schools from church domination.

---

[15] *Op. cit.*, II, p. 658.

Chapter III

THE Constitution of the United States guarantees two principles of religious freedom. Citizens need not support an established church, nor must they profess a specific religious faith in order to participate in their government. For a time religious freedom thus defined applied to the national government alone. Individual states might still maintain an established church and impose requirements of religious belief and religious tests for office upon their citizens. Indeed, as we have seen, this is precisely what a number of states continued to do for some years after the adoption of the Federal Constitution. Not until the passage of the Fourteenth Amendment in 1868 and the Supreme Court's broad and liberal interpretation of its provisions, was the final step taken to assure religious freedom to all within the jurisdiction of the states as well as of the national government.[1] This amendment provides in part that "no state shall make or enforce any law which shall abridge the privileges or immunities of citizens of the United States, nor shall any state deprive any person of life, liberty or property without due process of law; nor deny

[1] For a helpful discussion of the relation of this amendment to religious freedom, see Charles A. Beard's *The Republic*, Chapter XII.

25

to any person within its jurisdiction the equal protection of its laws."

Decisions of the Supreme Court in recent years interpret this statement as guaranteeing freedom of speech, of press, and of religion without restriction by state legislatures and municipal governments. Freedom of conscience is thus secure as long as the Constitution endures, and Americans are reasonably safe from the evils of sectarian government.

But children are not full-fledged citizens, and for many generations following the legal separation of church and state, the schools of the country continued to instill sectarian doctrines in the minds of American boys and girls.

One explanation derives from the fact that education is not a specific function of the Federal Government. It is rather the concern of state and locality. Moreover, education as a state responsibility existed in 1787 only in the imagination of a rare individual. In practice all schooling was private and parochial. Nearly a century elapsed before public schools sustained by public funds became an actuality.

Nothing reveals more dramatically the hopes and aspirations of people at their best than the provision they make for education. Schools reflect what men out of their own experience most sincerely wish for their offspring. In the curriculum and the conduct of schools, often tardily to be sure, but nevertheless eventually, is written a people's conception of the essentials of the good life.

In the beginning these essentials were religious in character. Consequently the curriculum of the school was designed to equip young people with the ideas and the tools basic for meeting their religious needs. In New England, for example, the minister of the congregation was long charged with the responsibility of supervising instruction in the school. And, if we may judge from the inspiring content of children's literature, they were often the authors, as well, of the books from which the youthful mind derived its notions of man and the universe. Imagine, for example, the enthusiasm with which the Colonial child would view his future after reading that "thriller" written by the eminent divine, Cotton Mather, entitled, "A Token for the Children of New England, or some examples of children in whom the feare of God was remarkably budding when they died in several parts of New England"! Or the sense of progress the earnest young seeker after knowledge would acquire as he spelled out the "Last Words and Dying Expressions of Hannah Hill, aged eleven years and near three months."

Nor was the future beyond the grave, as portrayed in textbooks and recreational reading for the young, wisely calculated to stimulate a desire to flee from this vale of tears. Many a New England child suffered the agonies of the damned in his dreams at night, following a feverish reading of Wigglesworth's *Day of Doom,* with its description, literally believed by the faithful, of the manner in which the quick and the dead are one day to be summoned before the bar of eternal judgment.[2]

2 "Mean men lament, great men do rent their robes and tear their hair:
　They do not spare their flesh to tear through horrible despair.
　All kindreds wail; all hearts do fail: Horror the world doth fill
　With weeping eyes and loud out-cries, yet knows not how to kill."

To be sure, not all the colonies maintained schools identical with those of New England, nor were all religious sects as convinced as the Puritan that this world was solely to be eschewed. In sections where the Anglican Church dominated, more mellow and tolerant attitudes prevailed. But in these colonies—New York, Virginia, Maryland, Georgia, the Carolinas—schooling was virtually restricted to the upper classes. Here, too, the apprentice system laid its heavy hand upon the children of the lower classes, and it was a rare master indeed who concerned himself with the education of his apprentice in more than the bare essentials. Only here and there might one find a charity school affording a limited number of children the opportunity to learn reading and writing, some arithmetic, the catechism and the religious observances of the Church of England.[3]

In the Middle Colonies numerous sects settled in relatively homogeneous religious communities. These groups strove to provide schools for children of their own religious persuasion under the personal direction of the local clergyman.

Secondary education was secured either from private tutors or from the grammar school. The curriculum of the latter was limited to little more than Latin and Greek, basic alike for the aspiring clergyman and the gentleman. Instruction in both elementary and secondary education was authoritarian and dogmatic. Absent entirely was the modern emphasis upon original think-

[3] E. P. Cubberly, *Public Education in the United States.* Boston: Houghton Mifflin Co., 1919, p. 43.

ing, the acquisition of methods of study or controlled investigation, the weighing of evidence, the testing of conclusions. Pupils recited individually and according to the words of the text. Pike's arithmetic, for example, contained 360 rules to be mastered and recited upon without intelligible explanation.

Education of this character does not develop independence of mind. Consequently, it is not surprising to learn that superstitions abounded and ignorant conceptions of man and of nature prevailed. According to one historian:

"The popular imagination, edged by theology, was still under the spell of mediaeval science: 'moon-signs, zodiac-signs, horoscopes, ominous eclipses followed by devastating fires, and comets presaging disaster and the death of princes,' and the active meddling of grotesque evil spirits and house-haunting demons. Belief in witchcraft was the fashion of the time, the Puritans in particular fully accepting the Biblical injunction 'Thou shalt not suffer a witch to live.' The penal code of the period, which was marked by Mosaic and mediaeval barbarity, recognized differences in rank. Punishments fell less heavily upon the well-to-do than upon the inferior." [4]

What accounts for the transformation of education from these meager beginnings into the American public school of today, a school free to all and dedicated to the heroic task of meeting the needs of boys and girls of different backgrounds, talents, and life goals?

[4] Edgar W. Knight, *Education in the United States*. Boston: Ginn and Company, 1929, p. 91.

A first step was the enrichment of the curriculum of both elementary and secondary schools in response to the secular needs of a growing middle class. As men pushed back the frontier, cleared the forests and broke new land, improved roads, bettered means of transportation, and developed a small business and industry, they came to see in education a valuable tool for attaining material comforts; and the school as a result began gradually to diminish its other-worldly emphasis. Education followed the changing pattern of American life and men's increasing realization that all is not evil in the "world of the flesh and the devil."

Most conspicuous in this evolution of the school was the rise of the American academy, the forerunner of the present high school. Prominent amongst the founders of this distinctively American institution was Benjamin Franklin, who sketched plans for an academy in Philadelphia as early as 1743. When this academy was finally launched, the trustees indicated clearly to the public the need of educating native-born Americans, who might thus qualify themselves to compete with foreigners in public and commercial employment.[5] And, with a practical eye toward possible sources of support, they stated: "It is thought that a good Academy erected in Philadelphia, a healthy place where Provisions are plenty, situated in the Center of the Colonies, may draw a number of students from the neighboring Provinces, who must spend Considerable Sums yearly among us, in Payment for their Lodging, Diet, Apparel, &c., which will

[5] See Elmer Ellsworth Brown, *The Making of Our Middle Schools.* New York: Longmans, Green & Co., 1914, pp. 185ff.

be an advantage to our Traders, Artisans, and Owners of Houses and Lands."

The broad purposes of the American academy are strikingly illustrated in the "constitution" of Andover at the time of its founding in 1778. This states that the donors intend "to lay the broad foundations of a public free school or academy for the purpose of instructing youth, not only in English and Latin, Grammar, Writing, Arithmetic, and those Sciences wherein they are commonly taught; but more especially to learn them the *Great End or Real Business of Living.*" With respect to the specific functions the academy was to serve, the constitution indicates that "the *first* and *principal* object of this institution is the promotion of true Piety and Virtue; the *second,* instruction in English, Latin, and Greek Languages, together with Writing, Arithmetic, Music, and the art of Speaking; the third, practical Geometry, Logic, and Geography; and the fourth, such other of the liberal Arts and Sciences or Languages, as opportunity and ability may hereafter admit, and as the Trustees shall direct."

Academies spread rapidly throughout the country, ministering ever more generously to the needs of young people who sought an education and training appropriate to the vocations and professions, and to the responsibilities of citizenship, in a rapidly expanding country. In New York, for example, in 1837, some seventy-five subjects were taught in the academies of the state! •

6 "Arithmetic, algebra, architecture, astronomy, botany, bookkeeping, Biblical antiquities, biography, chemistry, composition, conic sections, constitution of the United States, constitution of New York, elements of criticism, declamation, drawing, dialing, English grammar, evidences of

An inspection of these offerings will reveal the variety of occupations as well as the intellectual interests for which schools undertook to prepare their students. Preparation for the ministry and a sound grounding in the principles of Christianity were still prominent objectives, but they no longer monopolized education as they did in the Colonial period.

Closely allied to the economic motive in broadening education was the civic and political. The American Revolution freed the colonies from England, but the common man had still to win political independence. Following the adoption of the Constitution came manhood suffrage, and with the individual's participation in government—local, state, and national—the need for the education of political intelligence became obvious. Fortunately, conservative and radical alike agreed that education was indispensable for good government. Those who feared the people urged public support of education, as did Governor Holmes of North Carolina in 1824, on the theory that "knowledge, well and generally diffused amongst every class of our citizens . . . will enable them to resist all innovations of Demagogues or am-

---

Christianity, embroidery, civil engineering, extemporaneous speaking, French, geography, physical geography, geology, plane geometry, analytic geometry, Greek, Grecian antiquities, German, general history, history of the United States, history of New York, Hebrew, Italian, Latin, law (constitutional, select revised statutes, criminal, mercantile, Blackstone's Commentaries), logic, leveling, logarithms, vocal music, instrumental music, mapping, mensuration, mineralogy, mythology, natural history, navigation, nautical astronomy, natural theology, orthography, natural philosophy, moral philosophy, intellectual philosophy, penmanship, political economy, painting, perspective, physiology, English pronunciation, reading, rhetoric, Roman antiquities, stenography, statistics, surveying, Spanish, trigonometry, topography, technology, principles of teaching."
—From Alexander Inglis, *Principles of Secondary Education*. Boston: Houghton Mifflin Co., 1918, p. 180.

bitious men, whose views to the constitution are inimical or subversive." [7] On the other hand, labor leaders and liberal-minded citizens generally looked to education as a means for enabling the common man to capitalize upon the inexhaustible opportunities of a land in which "every man is king."

These broader concerns of the school both encouraged and pointed to the need for public support of education. Under the influence of French thought, and the stimulus of the open road to opportunity in America, states both south and north undertook to provide free elementary schools and to subsidize private secondary schools. Jefferson's plans for education in Virginia, devised in 1779, were not adopted as formulated, but they testified, nevertheless, to the revolution in men's minds with respect to education. In France, Diderot wrote, "A university is a school which is open without discrimination to all the children of a nation, where masters paid by the state initiate them into the elementary knowledge of all the sciences." In the United States men of like persuasion labored to give reality to this theoretical formulation of principle. Thus arose our early state school systems. At first, and in some quarters, the stigma of the charity school tended to inhibit these early endeavors, but the sale of public lands in the west and the gradual establishment of school funds out of public lands tended to transform schools into co-operative community enterprises, toward which the boastful American quite properly "pointed with pride."

[7] Quoted by Howard K. Beale, *A History of Freedom of Teaching in American Schools* (Report of the Commission on the Social Studies, Part XVI). New York: Charles Scribner's Sons, 1941, pp. 65–66.

Public support of education led naturally to the suggestion that the state, in a country where church and state are separate, should not further the interests of one religious sect as against another. This emphasis upon religious neutrality expressed itself differently on different levels of education and in different localities.

One way, as we have seen, was to develop state systems of education under public control and supported entirely by public funds. Another was to subsidize private schools and to insure a wider degree of public control and public service through the process of broadening representation on boards of trustees and liberalizing the curriculum of sectarian schools. Indeed, so strong was this nonsectarian spirit that state legislatures on occasion refused to grant charters for the establishment of schools that proposed to restrict their privilege to the adherents of but one religious faith. The Missouri legislature, for example, approved in 1834 a charter for academies at Troy and Independence, Missouri, on condition only that "no preference shall be given or any discrimination made [in the choice of trustees, professors, teachers, or students] on account of religious sentiments; nor shall any trustees, professors or teachers, at any time, make by-laws, ordinances or regulations that may, in any wise, interfere with or in any manner control the conscience, or the free exercise of religious worship." [8] Other states adopted similar measures, in the attempt to limit sectarian instruction even within schools that stemmed from sectarian groups.

It was natural, in this atmosphere, for states to ex-

[8] *Ibid.*, p. 94.

clude sectarian instruction from schools supported in whole or in part by public funds. And thus it became common practice throughout the nation for state constitutions to prohibit the use of public funds on behalf of institutions that engaged in sectarian instruction.

But what constitutes sectarian instruction? Words acquire their meaning from a context, and context varies with time and place. Prior to the Civil War and the Reconstruction Period the term nonsectarian encompassed what was common to Protestant sects, e.g., acceptance of the Protestant Bible and belief in the Protestant God and forms of worship common to Protestant sects. During this period Protestant parochial schools found it increasingly difficult to finance an education that was confined exclusively to members of their own denominations. Consequently, they hit upon the device of opening their doors to children of other creeds. This more generous admissions policy naturally tended to shift emphasis in religious instruction from points of difference to items of common agreement as between Protestants. By the time public schools, publicly supported, developed in great numbers, the principle of nonsectarian religious teaching was quite generally established.

This represented a most significant step in American education and American culture, since it immediately preceded immigration on a large scale from non-Protestant countries. As we shall see in a moment, the presence of increasing numbers of Catholics and Jews and other religious minorities in our population subjected principles of tolerance and fair play to severe strain. Children of "foreigners" suffered severely in school, on the playground, and on the street. Nonsectarian religious instruction was inadequate to meet this difficulty, but it solved the problem of religious diversity for the moment and constituted the basis for a still more generous policy in the future. For the time being, the nonsectarian emphasis seemed to insure an appropriate emphasis upon religion and morality in the schools while safeguarding children from the ill effects of sectarian rivalry.

No sooner was this remedy devised, however, than the problem took on a new and puzzling character. Following the Civil War, and continuing well into the first decades of the present century, our population underwent significant changes. Western Europe, and particularly Protestant Europe, ceased to furnish the vast majority of our immigrants. New and strange peoples with new and strange religious views found in America a haven and a refuge not unlike that which originally attracted our "native American stock." As soon as these new groups succeeded in rooting themselves firmly in American life, they began to demand for themselves and their children equality of treatment and fair play in social and political life.

Nor was equality easily attained. The harsh and inconsiderate treatment accorded the children of Jehovah's Witnesses in some communities today is but a faint reproduction of far more stern and uncompromising handling of Catholic and Jewish children seventy-five to one hundred years ago. In Boston, in 1858, a Catholic child was severely whipped when it refused to read the

Protestant Bible.[9] About the same time one hundred Catholic children were expelled from a Boston school as a penalty for refusing to participate in religious exercises. And in the city of brotherly love an irate mob burned Catholic schools, in answer to a Catholic bishop's suggestion that the public schools excuse Catholic children from the necessity of reading the Protestant version of the Bible.[10]

For a time Catholic and Jewish objection to the exposure of their children to the Protestant religion received little sympathy from either people at large or the courts of the country. In 1844, during the period of Native-Americanism and Know-Nothingism, a convention of Presbyterians and Congregationalists declared: "The liberty to *worship* God according to the dictates of conscience, conceded to our citizens by the Constitution, by any principle of legitimate interpretation, cannot be construed into a right to embarrass the municipal authorities of this Christian and Protestant nation in the ordering of their district schools." [11] And as late as 1898, an annotation of the Wisconsin statutes asserted that the constitutional prohibitions against sectarian teaching referred only "to religious doctrines that are believed by some religious sects and rejected by others," but "to teach the existence of a supreme being of infinite wisdom, power and goodness and that it is the duty of all men to adore, obey and love him, is not sectarian because all religious sects so believe and teach." [12]

9 *Ibid.*, p. 102.
10 *Ibid.*, p. 101
11 *Loc. cit.*
12 *Ibid.*, p. 211.

Gradually, however, rifts appeared in the ranks of the intolerant. In 1872 the Cincinnati Board of Education forbade the reading of the Bible in the schools of the city. The Supreme Court of Wisconsin ruled in 1890 that the reading of the Bible in schools was unconstitutional; and in 1902, 1910, and 1915 the supreme courts of Nebraska, Illinois, and Louisiana respectively rendered decisions of a similar nature, holding that both the reading of the Bible and hymn singing constituted sectarian instruction and acts of worship within the meaning of the state constitution. Gradually these efforts began to bear fruit and, whereas, for example, as late as 1903 ten states still required the reading of the Bible in the schools, by 1913 only two retained mandatory provisions of this character.

The attitude of Catholics with respect to religious services is interesting. Since to them religion constitutes a major part of education, it was difficult for them to object to religious instruction as such. Neither could they sanction a procedure whereby their children or teachers of their faith were required to use the Protestant Bible and to engage in services which violated religious conviction. Here and there attempts were made to excuse Catholic children from religious services, but this had the disadvantage of obviously pointing the finger of deviation at them and resulted often in unfortunate incidents. Efforts were likewise made to secure special appropriations out of tax receipts for parochial schools. Since this latter course (still an officially approved policy of Catholics) ran the danger of destroying public schools and of stimulating the growth of sectarian schools, it too was unsuccessful.

Indeed, so general was public opposition to this solution that President Grant, in his message of December 7, 1875, proposed the adoption of an amendment to the Constitution of the United States which would forbid the teaching of religious tenets and the granting of any school funds or school taxes "either by legislative, municipal, or other authority, for the benefit or in aid, directly or indirectly, of any religious sect or denomination."

Under these circumstances and since, in common with Americans generally, they wished teachers of their own faith to enjoy the privilege of teaching in public schools, Catholics joined liberal-minded Protestants, atheists, and Jews in the attempt to banish the Bible and religious instruction from the public school.

To fair-minded Americans this solution seemed to harmonize with the democratic principle of equal respect for differences. Consequently, as the country expanded and towns and cities of mixed population grew in numbers, it became customary to exclude religion from the school. Indeed, so common was this practice that an observer of American life in 1900 would undoubtedly have predicted the early demise of sectarian and nonsectarian instruction alike. Nevertheless, as Howard K. Beale remarks, "the whole question was badly confused. Still there was much less Bible reading in 1900 than in 1880, and less in 1910 than in 1900. . . . Fifty years ago in homogeneous Protestant communities prohibition of all religious exercises would have denied most teachers and pupils a generally desired privilege. At the end of this period, removal of the whole matter from the schools probably coerced fewer teachers and pupils into practices to which they objected than would any other solution." [13]

A number of factors thus explain the emergence of the secular school. Taken together they constitute the secular spirit of American life. In part this is nothing other than the spirit of fair play—the application of the Golden Rule to religious differences and the conviction that it is wrong to force one's private religious views upon a neighbor's children. In part the secular spirit reflects the material well-being in which the mass of Americans have come to share, and the competition between life values to which this well-being gives rise. Religion, in the sense of dogmatic adherence to a specific creed, no longer dominates the minds of people at large. Other values have come to soften and mellow the outlook, and to render more sensitive the associations of people in home and community life. The narrow religionists bemoan this greater diffusion of attention; others see in it one essential for creating urbane and civilized relations between individuals whose cultures constitute a coat of many colors in a closely knit world. Also contributing to the secular spirit are the influence of science, particularly the theory of evolution, with its devastating effects upon traditional theology, and the rise of historical criticism and the transformation thus effected in people's conception of the Bible. As Conrad

[13] *Ibid.,* p. 218.

Moehlman has put it, "the Bible which disappeared from the classroom as a religious text in the late nineteenth century *has also disappeared from history*. The dogmatic Bible of yesterday has evolved into the historical Bible of today." [14]

These are some of the factors that have completely transformed American education in little more than one hundred and fifty years. The American school began as a private and a parochial enterprise designed to perpetuate the religious and dogmatic conceptions of a religious denomination. Today education is primarily a public enterprise. Its support is public and its purposes are to serve ever better the needs of all the people. Originating as a private and a sectarian school, it evolved slowly into, first, a nonsectarian school for Protestants, and finally, the secular institution of today.

This secular school is now under fire. Powerful influences are attempting to annul the principle of separation of church and state and to bring religion back into the curriculum. Let us examine the causes for this reversion to the past and the consequences which may follow upon a counterrevolution of this character.

---

[14] See in this connection Professor Moehlman's challenging chapter, "Can the Bible Return to the Classroom?" (*op. cit.*, pp. 103–122).

Chapter IV

B Y 1914 the secular school seemed firmly established in the United States. The eighteenth century had brought freedom to the Colonies and the separation of church from state. The nineteenth developed a public school free of access to the children of all the people without discrimination. In so far as the state and the public could insure it, the children of every religious sect, or no sect at all, might mingle hereafter as equals in the public school, and there come to know and respect each other as individuals. Thus unwittingly, a foundation was laid in attitudes of tolerance and respect with which to resolve in later years even greater divergences of religion and race and nationality. There was reason to hope that immigrants from all parts of the world might become one people through their children—with the assistance of the public school.

This, I repeat, was the promise and often the realization of the American public school in the early years of the twentieth century. And while more than one state and locality constituted islands of exception, in which attitudes of exclusiveness and 100 per cent Americanism of the good old Protestant and northern European variety were carefully preserved, it is fair to say that American education faced the future and a changing world with confidence and assurance.

Then came World War I. As James Truslow Adams wrote in his *Epic of America:* "The earth, which we had thought safe and solid to work and play and dream our dreams on, suddenly sank beneath our feet. The waves closed over all that had been known and familiar and loved. The lights of the world went out."

The first World War ended in 1918. Few people foresaw at the time that a war to end war and "to make the world safe for democracy" was but a prelude to a second world war on a far larger scale, or that the period intervening would witness a steady disintegration of nerve within the western democracies, an undermining of democratic principles and practices, a reversion to authoritarianism in men's minds as well as in government. But this is precisely what came about. The mood in which the people of the United States entered the postwar period was altogether different from that immediately preceding the war. Gone were the optimism and enthusiasm with which they viewed their own institutions, and that sense of inner security which enables men to welcome the unknown. Scarcely was the Armistice signed, before the "softening up process" of fear and doubt and intolerance began to operate in this country as well as in the nations that later constituted the Axis powers.

The earliest symptom of reversion in politics took the form of a "return to normalcy," a retreat from the position of international leadership that this country had assumed under Woodrow Wilson. In defeating Wilson's attempt to take this country into the League of Nations, the Senate committed the United States to a policy of narrow and futile isolationism and blocked the healthy evolution of an international organization of nations.

But isolationism could not safeguard Americans from influences which begat a Fascist and Nazi spirit abroad or from outbreaks of fanaticism and intolerance at home. What Hitler was to Germany, the Huey Longs strove to become to the United States. Authoritarianism here took the form of demagogic appeals to the masses to "share the wealth" and alleviate the insecurities and hardships of poverty in return for a surrender of civil and political liberties. Within the social as well as the political field sinister groups organized themselves as Ku Klux Klans and Black Legions. Other associations took unto themselves labels designed to identify their members in the eyes of the naïve as "Christian soldiers" fighting for a pure America. These enemies of democracy set out to realize a Protestant and a white America by excluding from the privileges of our common life Catholics and Jews, "atheists," Negroes, and "foreigners."

Following a brief and highly intoxicating period of prosperity in the Twenties, came the depression of the Thirties. The sufferings engendered by unemployment, and the resulting cutthroat competition of man against man for the privilege of earning one's daily bread, tended further to undermine men's confidence in time-honored principles of democracy as well as men's generous attitudes toward differences in race, color, and creed. To which was added the deliberate attempt of propagandists from abroad to stir up hate and fear in our population and thus to keep our people divided, uncertain, afraid.

Economic conservatives feared the depression might wash out the system of private enterprise. Nor were the capitalists themselves, in this period, overly confident of the strengths and the virtues of the capitalistic system. For example, in the darkest days of the depression an attorney of a large corporation operating in the financial district of New York remarked that nowhere had he encountered graver criticisms of capitalism than in Wall Street itself! Under these circumstances, it was natural for men who wished to salvage the *status quo* to turn for help to the two institutions which might most easily secure its underpinnings: the school and the church.

Efforts to control education were evident in the sensitiveness of conservative citizens and organized groups about the content of history and economics in schools and colleges, and in attempts to black out information on Russia and the Communist Revolution. Pressure groups attacked the use of scholarly histories because of fear of the effects that truth might have on the minds and the attitudes of the young. Particularly objectionable to these people were the trend toward realism in teaching and the use of original source materials dealing with the economic development of America.[1]

Religion too gave evidence of loss of nerve. Prior to the war, and for a brief interval thereafter, the Social Gospel movement waxed strong, testifying to a spirit of confidence in man and man's ability through cooperative efforts to create a tolerable habitation on this

[1] See, for example, the attacks on Harold Rugg's textbooks.

earth. This trend in religious thought found adherents in all churches, Protestant, Catholic, and Jewish alike, and served to offset in a measure the traditional individualistic emphasis found in Christianity. In contrast to the ancient injunction to render unto Caesar the things that are Caesar's and to eschew the good things of this world, it stressed the importance of establishing the Kingdom of God on earth. The Social Gospel movement was optimistic in spirit, confident of man's capacity to better his environment and to transform his own nature. It tended to discount the importance of creedal differences and to emphasize instead a spirit of secular concern for the conditions of the good life here and now—even though the nature of this good life was none too clearly defined.

The depression and the steady retreat of democracy in Europe before the onslaughts of Fascism, with a resulting loss of confidence in our own political and economic institutions, brought a rapid change in religious outlook in America. Reinhold Niebuhr's *Moral Man and Immoral Society* was typical of the change. In this book Niebuhr voiced skepticism of man's power to check progressively the egoism of individuals or to develop a religiously inspired good will that might eventually "establish social harmony between all the human societies and collectives." Man's evil nature and the essential stubbornness of his original nature in group relationships were reaffirmed. Other religious thinkers were also quick to abandon ship and to join in a counterrevolution under the banner of a Neo-orthodoxy. Often the identical individuals who in the early Twenties had issued a clarion call for social reconstruction in the name of religion now characterized such efforts as evidence of man's "pride and egoism"; or, as one of their number expresses it, they began to see

"that in their endeavor to 'modernize' and 'liberalize' Christianity they had brought it into a compromising alliance with the peculiar presuppositions, prejudices and illusions of a particular type of civilization (Western industrialism) and even of a particular section of society (the middle class). Since this particular type of civilization has begun to suffer a decline, and since this particular section of society has passed its apogee, the liberal theology has now fallen beneath the same sentence of doom which it so often pronounced upon older systems of theology: O irony of ironies, its 'thought forms' have become 'outmoded.' " [2]

With this change of mood came the tendency to flee from the concerns of this world and to make one's peace with God, since man himself can do little to effect salvation. Gone were the efforts of some years ago to define God in terms of a quickened social conscience which expresses itself in man's efforts to attain his highest. In contrast, God was represented as removed from the affairs of men, sanctioning, if not encouraging, a like complacency on the part of man with respect to an unjust world order.

Reaction and retreat in religion in recent years are no longer restricted to the theologians. Within the ranks of the common people a phenomenal number of religious sects of an evangelical and millenarian variety

[2] Walter Marshall Horton, *Theology in Transition*. New York: Harper & Brothers, 1943, Part II, p. 5.

have sprung up. Writing in the *Survey Graphic* of June 1944, Eduard Lindeman calls attention to the rapid multiplication of these sects in the Middle West. Of them, he states:

"The theological tendency seems to be in the direction of Christian millenarianism which is based upon belief in the Second Coming of Christ. I heard a startling interpretation of this doctrine from a preacher in a large church in Dallas, Texas, in which he stated that the world is to pass through seven stages of degeneration, all precisely prophesied in the Old Testament; we are now in the midst of the fifth stage of degeneration; obviously, Christ cannot return until this cycle has been completed and consequently those who now strive to improve the world through remedial measures automatically postpone the Second Coming. These reformers are, then, the evil ones and must be kept in subjection through some form of authority.

"Until I had heard this weird doctrine, I had experienced considerable difficulty in understanding how these fundamentalists could possibly hate so many enemies. I had listened to attacks upon Jews, Negroes, sympathizers with Negroes, trade union leaders, New Dealers, progressive educators, and so on, and now I began to comprehend the reasons for so long a list. Anybody who impedes the Second Coming is *ipso facto* anti-Christ." [3]

I do not intend to imply that all the forces of religion in the period between two world wars breathed a spirit of defeat. Obviously this is not the case. Many religious leaders continued to preach the Gospel of hope and of courage. My point is that these trying years, particularly

[3] *Survey Graphic*, XXXIII (June, 1944), pp. 280–282.

the depression years, brought to large numbers of people, the intelligentsia as well as the run-of-the-mine individual, the conviction that our civilization is in process of disintegration. With this conviction the Americans' traditional optimism began to evaporate, and attention began to shift from what is essential to better man's lot on the earth below to the conditions of salvation in the heavens above.

II

And what of education? What hope and sustenance for the spiritual fiber of American society emanated from the schools in this period?

Public education in the early decades of the century confronted a Herculean task. It had both to assimilate large numbers of young people, including children of recent immigrants, to American life, and to ease the growing pains of a population in process of transition from a predominantly rural and agricultural economy to a new industrial society. Since in America class lines were fluid and each generation hoped to better its station in life, this process involved equipping a rapidly expanding school population with the information, the skills, and the techniques that were essential for new vocational opportunities. These opportunities were more and more attached to industrialization. Horace Greeley's injunction, "Go West, young man!" no longer carried the weight of former years. Large cities rather than the open country of the West served as a magnet for the ambitious.

Immigration and industrialization thus defined the

problem of public education in the first quarter of the century. The immediate effect was a rapid increase in school enrollments. Not only did the total number of children of school age grow with leaps and bounds, but the proportion of children of elementary and secondary school age likewise multiplied rapidly. Schooling, in other words, became an open sesame for success in life as it had not been formerly.

School administrators, confronted with the necessity of accommodating a rapidly growing student body—to say nothing of educating it effectively—centered upon the expansion of building facilities, materials, and supplies, as well as a teaching personnel trained in methods of teaching designed to insure tangible and efficient results in large class groups. Considering the fact that this teaching personnel was drawn in large numbers from the selfsame groups which were undergoing assimilation into American life, the task was difficult indeed.

The solution of these problems was sought in mass education and in a gradual shift from qualitative to quantitative standards in teaching. Teachers were encouraged, if not required, to concentrate upon the externals of teaching, to the neglect of the inner life of the child. Harassed superintendents of schools and supervisors turned to scientific management for suggestions, with the result that not only administrative and supervisory procedures but also the organization of courses of study came to reflect the principles derived from large-scale business organizations.

Writing in 1933, a group of educators had this to say of education in this period:

"For centuries education has been identified with the use of books. On its lowest level it has centered upon abolishing illiteracy and upon helping people to acquire the rudiments of reading and writing. On the higher levels of learning it has envisaged culture as an external acquisition: as primarily an entering into those aspects of racial inheritance which are easily perpetuated in books.

"This encourages administrators to oversimplify the educational process; to view the school as an organization devoted to the dispensing of ready-made knowledge, much as a wholesale establishment prepares and assorts packages for distribution, grading them according to the needs of different types of consumers. Moreover, the tools put forth by scientific education in the period under review were well adapted to reinforce this trend. Intelligence tests seemed to hold forth the possibility of classifying children in terms of their native abilities, while achievement tests revealed the extent to which children measured up to their powers. Job, activity and functional analyses in the hands of scientifically trained curriculum experts pointed to the specific performances in which children could engage and the specific information they could acquire in order to arrive at the specific ideas and to establish the specific responses essential for effective performance in a mechanized world. Behaviorism in psychology and the scientific study of education thus seemed to confirm the suggestion that business methods of organization and management be applied to school administration and supervision." [4]

As these authors suggest, the psychology of the hour seemed to reinforce and to justify an essentially mechanical approach to education.

[4] *The Educational Frontier* by William H. Kilpatrick [Ed.] and others. New York: The Century Co., 1933, pp. 225–226.

John Watson, for example, in his widely read book, *The Psychological Care of Infant and Child,* pointed to the dangers of too overt manifestation of love and affection on the part of parents. In order to safeguard children from oversentimental treatment and the injurious effects of a mother love that is essentially self-gratifying rather than selfless, he extolled the virtues of an objective and unaffectionate handling of children. Thus he writes:

"There is a sensible way of treating children. Treat them as though they were young adults. Dress them, bathe them with care and circumspection. Let your behavior always be objective and kindly firm. Never hug or kiss them, never let them sit in your lap. If you must, kiss them once on the forehead when they say goodnight. Shake hands with them in the morning. Give them a pat on the head if they have made an extraordinarily good job of a difficult task. Try it out. In a week's time you will find how easy it is to be perfectly objective with your child and at the same time kindly." [5]

And again:

"I sometimes wish that we could live in a community of homes where each home is supplied with a well-trained nurse so that we could have babies fed and bathed each week by a different nurse." [6]

Impelled by this scientific dictum, experts in child care proceeded to enjoin parents and teachers alike to discipline their natural affection, and homes and schools

[5] New York: W. W. Norton & Co., 1928, pp. 81–82.
[6] *Ibid.,* p. 83.

to adopt an impersonal and "objective" attitude toward children. Emphasis centered upon habit formation, upon bringing about conformity and regularity in behavior as outwardly viewed rather than upon the more subtle influences on the child's personality of an arm's-length method of transforming young animals into human beings.

To eat spinach when spinach was prescribed, to observe health habits, to follow the rulebooks on child care, were highly valued without a too tender consideration for the emotional and social attitudes thus engendered. Not until some years later did experiments establish the fact that children thrive on affection and are not altogether healthy emotionally without it, and that even the very young infant gains in weight and general health better in a warm affectionate atmosphere than in a cool and calm setting devoid of affection!

If authorities on child development could induce large numbers of parents to treat their children impersonally, how much more eagerly would the harassed and otherwise conscientious teachers of oversized classes welcome the injunctions of the psychologist! To them science became a veritable balm for hurt minds, since it reduced teaching to an external manipulation of subject matter scientifically selected and presented in conformity with patterns drawn from experiments on controlled groups of children.

Both curricular materials and teaching methods thus came under the domination of scientific psychology. This psychology rested on assumptions which became for a time veritable dogmas in education. And bold indeed was the textbook writer or the educational practitioner who ventured to deviate therefrom!

The most pertinent of these assumptions were as follows: First, that all learning is habit formation—from the simplest reflex action (an hereditary habit) to the most complex and difficult conclusion of creative thought. Moreover, habits were viewed as composites of specific responses in the nervous system, which are closely related to situations in the environment. These "connections or bonds" between the situation and response were commonly designated as $S \rightarrow R$ bonds to which every act, thought, or emotion is reducible. Second, units of response are *specific;* from which it follows that all learning is specific. Each novel act that an individual performs flows from the fact that responses made in the past reappear in a new context or a new organization. Nothing really new is ever learned. The familiar serves always as a bridge to the unfamiliar. And it behooves the wise teacher, when instructing the learner in new facts or in the acquisition of new skills, to expedite his identification of old elements. In the phraseology of the day, there is no transfer of training other than by way of elements of experience that are present alike in the known and the unknown. Third—as a deduction from these two assumptions—a child's development must be closely supervised. Education requires control and direction from outside the learner. This premise applies not only to the relatively simple types of education, such as the mastery of the 1,235 "facts" into which primary arithmetic might be reduced, but likewise to the teaching of life's ideals. As a contemporary authority put it, when writing on the teaching of ideals, "Conduct and behavior are specific. . . . One does not act honestly in general; he performs a thousand specific acts of honesty. He tells the truth about the sharpened tool he ruined, about the dime lost, or about the window he broke in play. By an accumulation and integration of these thousand acts, he becomes an honest person." [7] Consequently, he who would develop character in young people must deal in specifics. Analyze the virtues we would have children acquire into the specific traits of which these virtues are composed, and then select the situations best calculated to fuse the two. To quote our authority again:

" 'Honor thy father and thy mother . . .' is an easy Commandment to memorize, but often the glibbest parrot in a church school has not the faintest idea of how to put the principle into practice. Children have to be taught these trait actions one by one. Only in a series can pupils learn to apply a principle. The individual actions must be patiently taught them. At one time they must learn to honor their father and mother by saying: 'Yes, Father'; at another time by placing the mother's chair; or at still a third time by offering the father the favorite seat. No mere knowledge of the general rule or deep desire to follow the ideal is a substitute for this detailed training in specific forms of action." [8]

The author of this quotation recognized that specific acts which are prompted by emotion and thought tend to come to a head eventually in a principle or an ideal of behavior, which in turn may initiate and direct action.

[7] W. W. Charters, *The Teaching of Ideals*. New York: The Macmillan Co., 1927, p. 106.
[8] *Ibid.*, pp. 107–108.

Less discerning students of conduct were not so tolerant of the function of ideals and principles in teaching. Indeed they viewed the latter as useless verbal luggage, as abstract and collective nouns, serving a convenient purpose in discourse, but lacking potency and reality apart from the particulars they designate. The real business of education centered upon developing in children the myriads of specific responses essential in their finding their way around in a world of discrete and specific events.

This psychology of learning carried an inherent appeal to superintendents of schools and supervisors charged with the grave responsibility of directing inadequately trained teachers in the art of teaching large class groups. The steps required for instruction were clear and definite. Bring together in manageable form, it was said, the relevant and pertinent facts and skills and statements of the abilities which children are to acquire; provide teachers with suggestions for inculcating these facts and skills; and then test from time to time the effectiveness with which both teacher and children have followed the plans thus formulated. Do this faithfully, and efficient results will follow.

Accordingly textbook writers and bureaus of educational research set about the task of determining *what* to teach, of organizing these details into specific instructions for teaching, and of devising instruments for testing the results of learning and teaching.

On the other hand, observe the responsibilities education thus assumed! All of life must be analyzed into its simple components; traits of mind and character which children should acquire are to be identified and classified, and ways and means devised for inducing the latter to make these traits their own! Nevertheless, as one industrious worker put it:

"The central theory is simple. Human life, however varied, consists in the performance of specific activities. Education that prepares for life is one that prepares definitely and adequately for these specific activities. . . . This requires only that one go out into the world of affairs and discover the particulars of which these affairs consist. These will show the abilities, attitudes, habits, appreciations, and forms of knowledge that men need. These will be the objectives of the curriculum. They will be numerous, definite, and particularized. The curriculum will then be that series of experiences which children and youth must have by way of attaining those objectives." [9]

Obvious benefits followed from this insistence upon definiteness and specificity. The pre-scientific era in education had encouraged the accumulation of much useless subject matter and questionable methods. The new emphasis was practical. Each item of subject matter was required to present its credentials before securing employment. Directly or indirectly it was required to further a specific item of knowledge or trait of character which clearly pointed the way toward effective adult life.

This practical approach was of benefit alike to the young and inexperienced teacher in a crowded schoolroom and to the children who were taught under this

[9] Franklin Bobbitt, *The Curriculum*. Boston: Houghton Mifflin Co., 1918, p. 42.

unfavorable condition. Many of the latter were either foreign born or the offspring of foreign born. An analysis of their requirements in the way of fact and skill, of personal habit and social outlook, gave relevance to school activities that might otherwise have been lacking. The traditional gap between school and community was partially bridged.

Nor was "job analysis" limited to elementary and secondary education. Under the influence of W. W. Charters, Stephens College in Missouri, a junior college for girls, undertook an analysis of the activities in which women engage and the problems and the needs they encounter in their daily lives. These fell into seven areas (communication, physical health, mental health, aesthetics, social adjustment, economics, religion). With areas of needs thus identified, the faculty strove to adapt and to make over courses of study with an eye to enabling students to acquire the principles and facts and skills that were essential for their functioning adequately as women. Other colleges soon followed suit, with the result that institutions of higher education began to furnish both men and women students much new wine, even though the bottles in which it was served frequently retained old labels.

On the other hand, the attempt to reduce all education to specific objectives loosened an avalanche of trivial and superficial research. Job analysis, so fruitful in certain areas of vocational education, particularly of a routine character, became a model for identifying the total content and method of education. Values acquired importance only as statistics established this importance, and quantitative standards tended to submerge considerations of quality.

For example, the teachers in one widely publicized school system attempted to determine through "research" the appropriate subject matter for an elementary course in history. This they did by noting carefully in periodicals of the day the allusions to historical and geographical items and weighing their importance for children by their frequency of mention. Other investigators patiently counted the items of scientific fact mentioned in popular publications, as a basis for determining the content of textbooks in science. Similarly with other subjects of the curriculum.

The extreme to which this busy work in education was in fact carried may be seen from the following application of the "law of deficiencies" in building a course in civics:

"On the assumption that newspaper and magazine editors, on the whole, point out civic and social deficiencies which need to be remedied, and hence might form the core of discussion in civic courses, the editorials of nine widely scattered but representative newspapers on the odd-numbered dates for a period of three months, and of six magazines for a period of four years, were examined to find everything pointed out by the editors as undesirable. . . . The deficiencies thus discovered were classified into four general groups: those of the private citizen, of various governmental units, of certain social groups, and of officials. The specific deficiencies of citizenship as found were then brought together as subclassifications under each of the general headings, and their frequency of occurrence was tabulated. Reflection on these deficiencies as listed revealed that certain objectives emerged characteristic of each general group of deficiencies and also that there emerged a set of objectives common to all the general groups. These were stated as abilities, habits, attitudes, dispositions, etc., and listed as specific objectives for civic teaching." [10]

There remained, for the assiduous students, only the task of discovering, selecting, and organizing the subject matter and methods best calculated to realize these objectives!

A moment ago I called attention to the assumptions which underlie this scientific movement in education. Nothing is left to chance. Initiative and originality are denied the learner. Accordingly the adult discharges his responsibility as parent or teacher only when he subjects the child to meticulous supervision and direction. This urge for control leads to a curious contradiction in practice. In seeking to determine young people's needs statistically, the requirements of a specific group of young people in a specific school setting are easily forgotten. In one college, for example, a study of freshman girls indicated letter-writing to be the most common writing activity. This suggested that training in letter-writing is a major task of the English teacher. In order to organize a sound course of this character the instructor analyzed letters written by women of distinction, as well as collections of letters written (in order to be specific!) by women only. From this emerged the ideals which should guide performance. Contrasted to these ideals were the weaknesses of students, as determined by

[10] L. A. Williams, *The Making of the High-School Curricula.* Boston: Ginn & Co., 1928, pp. 125–126.

an analysis of one thousand letters penned by college girls in their freshman year. The instructor now knew what to concentrate upon in his courses.—Evidently it did not occur to him that a sample or two of each student's writing might have yielded an equally pertinent list of evils sufficient unto the day thereof.

Irrelevance and waste of time are less serious faults than are mediocrity and a positive loss in spiritual values. "Science" in education was guilty of the triviality and superficiality which Abraham Flexner vigorously attacked some twenty years ago and which Chancellor Hutchins today now lustily condemns from each housetop. And in this both are justified.

They are justified since Gresham's law applies to education as well as to economic activity. Unsound currency inevitably drives the good out of circulation. So it came to pass in our schools that the intangible values, a concern for the significant things of life, an emphasis upon values in living other than the material and the commonplace, beat a steady retreat before the tangible and the ordinary.

Not all school systems, of course, prostrated themselves before the altar of the commonplace. Few succeeded, however, in freeing their classrooms utterly from the low level of educational concern thus generated. Moreover, textbooks took character, inevitably, from the dominant trend of the times, and only here and there did rugged individualists resist the influence in subject matter taught, or methods pursued, of the stimulus-response conception of education.

Let us bear in mind also the concern and the conviction, in these years, of powerful groups outside the school, with respect to the direction in which the young twig should bend. School administrators, ever mindful of these watchdogs, were driven by two fears. One derived from lack of faith in the professional competency of their teaching staffs. They doubted that the latter possessed the skill sufficient to cope constructively with complex issues, or, indeed, with the deep-seated growing-pains of young people. Second, they questioned their own ability to convince the public that rare educational possibilities reside within so-called "dangerous issues."

Driven by this fear and lack of confidence, school executives permitted education to drift with the current and to neglect values which did not lend themselves to easy counting. The result was that at one and the same time schools were giving increased emphasis to practical and material considerations, and neglecting or soft-pedaling attention to the more basic spiritual needs within the living tissue of young people's experience. To the extent that these needs received attention at all, it was in extracurricular activities or in experiences outside the jurisdiction of the school. Accordingly, young people lived two lives, one in the school and the classroom, and the other out of school. All too seldom did the first constitute a key of interpretation for the latter.

Obviously, schools which carefully avoid problems of life's meaning cannot raise up young people who are competent to gather the winds of experience in their fists. Nor will an education blind to the inner needs of young people satisfy the deep spiritual hungers of the times. American society, in the period under review, was a vast melting pot. While the tide of immigration which, in the last decades of the nineteenth century and the first decade of the twentieth, threatened to submerge the original American stock, was on the ebb, the first and second generations were still in process of assimilation. Neither the Daughters of the American Revolution nor the Ku Klux Klan nor political advocates of a return to normalcy could prevent change in traditional ideas, any more than they could maintain the "purity" of the original American stock. Whether they willed or no, a new society was in process of being born. The times invited a school bold enough to lead beyond the borders of the *status quo*. Young people who cried in their hearts for bread were not satisfied with a stone. Scientific education did not provide the meaning and the unity they sought to weave into their lives.

It was in part to correct these evils that progressive education came into being.

III

Early in the century, under the inspiration of John Dewey, the social potentialities of education received emphasis, in contrast to practices that had grown out of the traditional individualistic and atomistic conception of people in relation to each other. Dewey recognized that children attain emotional and social health as members of a community to which they give as well as receive. The original and the earliest concern of progressive education was thus both personal and social. It sought to make of the school a child's environment; to involve children in activities which prompt alike initiative

and resourcefulness and responsible social qualities. Nor
did the early progressive schools neglect the past. Rather
they sought to use the past so that children might comprehend how the present came to be. Indeed continuity
in education was an important theme—continuity between past and present, between school and community.
Accordingly, these schools endeavored, in Dewey's words,
"to bring about a definite integration of activities going
on in the larger community beyond the walls of the
school" so that young people might be brought into
"contact with the realities of present-day life." [11]

Here were the beginnings of a new kind of education,
one that might satisfy the requirements of a secular
school and at the same time educate for character. Indeed, in his little volume on *Moral Principles in Education*,[12] John Dewey outlined ways and means available
for training in moral character through the activities
of the classroom, in contrast to an exclusively verbal
emphasis.

Following 1918 a different spirit crept into progressive
schools. In many communities the progressive school
represented little more than a reaction against conventional and mass education. And, as so often happens, the
rebound from conformity was extreme nonconformity.
Mass education had cramped and confined the individual child. It caught him up in a lock-step performance,
requiring him to proceed with others at a uniform rate,
to learn identical items of information, or to perfect
identical skills in identical ways. Finally, mass educa-

[11] Chapter entitled "The Social-Economic Situation and Education," in
The Educational Frontier, pp. 33ff.
[12] Boston: Houghton Mifflin Co., 1909.

tion commonly required teachers to operate within an autocratically organized school system, in which not merely children followed orders "from above" but teachers likewise subordinated their individual talents to the dictation of higher authority.

Against all this, progressive education entered a vigorous protest. Children were recognized and treated as persons, each with a unique and distinct personality. This novel approach yielded immediate results. It revealed hitherto unsuspected possibilities within children. In a friendly and sympathetic atmosphere they astonished observers with original and creative productions. Children who had previously been passive and overly docile began to manifest initiative and self-direction. Subject matter, too, underwent change. As children's interests in the world about them became grist for the teacher's mill, young folks began to explore and inquire and investigate into their environment with a freshness of spirit and —within limits—with a thoroughness superior to that of the conventional school. And although the habits and skills and even the information thus acquired were often partial and lopsided, when laid against the standards of an adequate discipline, this condition disturbed not at all the nonconformist hearts of teachers who themselves were in rebellion against the old.

Out of the rebel nature of the teacher came the limitations of progressive education. All progressive educators united in opposition to lock-step conformity, excessive verbalism, and the woeful neglect of first-hand experience, characteristic of the conventional school. They recognized, with the mental hygienist and the new dynamic psychologist, the importance of emotional factors, not only in personality development but in the discipline of the mind; but they were not one on a positive program. This followed in part from the fact that the progressive school sympathized with and even aided and abetted the revolt of youth which came on the heels of the first World War.

The United States entered World War I on a wave of social idealism. Our people proposed to make the world safe for democracy and thus to extend to all mankind the benefits of a way of life they believed they had all but won for themselves. Wilson's first administration, as Theodore Roosevelt's before him, strove to make both natural and human resources available to the common man. And while industrial development, with its crude and often cruel neglect of the many who labored to produce riches for the few, obviously belied democratic professions, the spontaneous optimism of Americans ignored the difference between good intention and reality.

The conclusion of the war found Americans in a more sober mood. Young people who had cheerfully served their country abroad were disillusioned with the peace treaty and its aftermath. This spirit of disillusionment spread throughout the country, particularly amongst large numbers of able and competent young people, who now began to subject the old order to severe criticism.

Since it was from this group that progressive schools tended to draw both its teachers and its clientele, it is not surprising that it too should display the attributes of revolt. Opposition to regimentation and conformity

was identified with the right of a child not only to discover and explore his unique powers and abilities, but
to exercise his talents with little concern for his associates. Teachers who were social rebels at heart testified
to their faith by survival in the rough and tumble experiences of the "child centered" school. The individual-
ity of the child flourished rampantly, but opportunities
to grow in sensitive response to others, to realize the
supreme satisfaction which comes with the assumption
of another's burden, of being in fact a brother's keeper,
all too often lay fallow. Moreover, respect for the integrity of child nature at times assumed such exaggerated
proportions that the guidance which children hunger
for and require from sympathizing and understanding
adults was altogether lacking. In seeking to build secure
and rugged personalities, insecurities were generated.
Lest adult ideas be imposed upon young and impressionable minds, children were permitted to grow up ignorant
of their birthright in the form of identification with an
on-going tradition. The terms democracy and freedom
were often repeated, but fear of indoctrination rendered
adults timid in helping children to interpret and reorganize daily experience by reference to the moral principles which constitute the heart of democratic relations
between people.

Thus did the progressive school fail to capitalize upon
the character-forming possibilities inherent in an otherwise vital and meaningful education. Pathetic attempts
in conservative schools to teach morals by talking about
the moral virtues further confirmed the progressive
school in its opposition to anything resembling direct

moral instruction. The immediate life of the school and rich contacts with the community lent themselves to an interpretation from which young people might have evolved a democratic philosophy (formulated, of course, in children's terms), a faith to live by, as appealing and dramatic as that which many a hungry European youth discovered at the same time in Fascism and Communism. But the disposition to translate democracy into moral terms did not accord with the mood and spirit of the day.

IV

Thus for quite different reasons neither mass education nor progressive education measured up to its full responsibilities in the period between 1918 and the depression of the 1930's. Mass education failed because it could not see beyond the nose on its face. Its absorption in the mechanics and the specifics, the information and skills of a commonplace and mediocre variety, which all must acquire, caused it to ignore the far more vital task of helping young people to become in fact the architects of their own fortunes, to identify themselves creatively with both the materials and the methods essential for coping with the events and the circumstances of their lives. Mass education also played young people false in so far as it carefully avoided the growing pains alike of young people and their society. Controversial issues were sedulously excluded from the classroom: issues such as sex education (as much a problem of social relations between individuals in a changing society as a problem of personal development), the application of democratic principles to the existence of minorities, or the solution of social and economic problems of a people in process of transition to an industrial civilization.

Progressive education, being much closer to young people, enabled them to meet issues head on as they arose. But it lacked either a positive and clearly defined democratic philosophy or the courage to share this with others. Because of fear of imposing adult ideas upon the young, it often left them rudderless, without a tradition with which they could identify or guidance to direct their immature progress. Democracy thus became one with a species of rudderless individualism, which leaves the individual insecure at heart, since it confronts him with no opportunity to lose his life as a means of saving his own soul.

It required one of the severest depressions in our history to bring American education face to face with its essential tasks. Beginning roughly with 1930, three conspicuous changes manifested themselves in the work of the schools of the country, conservative and conventional as well as progressive.

First was the depression itself. It shocked educators into a realization that the school cannot operate in a vacuum, that children are influenced by forces which play upon them in the home and in the community and by the prevailing winds of the times. Economic, social, and psychological forces prescribe the task of the schools, setting limits and defining possibilities. Studies of the American Youth Commission seemed to indicate rapidly closing opportunities for youth. Not only did long-term trends indicate a lengthening out of the period of non-participation in economic activity for youth, a prolongation of the period of childhood and adolescence, but they demonstrated as well that the few who succeeded in receiving employment had less to look forward to in economic reward than in former days. The whole concept of adolescence thus required revision, suggesting for school and college alike modifications in the subject matter and method of teaching.

Second, the winnowing and sifting process of practice in working with children and adolescents within progressive schools and colleges yielded certain tangible results which were obvious to all educators. This experience testified to the advantages of both freedom and guidance. The modern teacher knows far more today than did his predecessors about childhood and youth, about the characteristics of growth and development at different age levels, and about ways in which young people can acquire habits of play and of work together and in the process a growing sensitiveness toward others and an essential self-respect. To this empirical knowledge has been added a fund of verifiable information on all phases of development—physical, emotional, social, intellectual—which are indispensable for progress toward maturity. Out of guidance clinics in school and college, mental hygiene institutes, research bureaus, and carefully controlled experiments has come a body of professional knowledge easily available to all. These studies, among other things, reveal the connection between inner and outer factors of growth and learning, the influence of economic circumstance and social status upon educational progress, the fateful effects of such things as parental attitudes on children, relations between brothers and sisters and playmates, the nourishing effects of acceptance, the destructive influence of rejection, the healthy influence of a sense of being needed.

Third, many schools have learned to translate these findings into school practices. They make conscious provision for meeting the needs of young people for affection, for assuring them that they belong to a group which both accepts them and depends upon them for clearly defined tasks. When so translated these basic essentials in education transform the administration and organization of school and classroom alike. Schools thus become communities in which teachers and young people and, in an increasing measure, parents share in common experiences and the evolution of common standards of living.

The character-transforming influence of this new approach is evident particularly where the school population is heterogeneous and diverse in composition. It has injected into these communities a spirit of unity and mutual acceptance that is basic for the moral and mental health of the young. Here initial differences in race and religion are not allowed to congeal into that haunting sense of difference which generates false notions of inferiority and superiority. In short, schools meet the first essential of intercultural education by giving body to the democratic principle that all men are more alike than different—a principle, incidentally, that must be *felt* as well as *known,* if it is to achieve results.

Schools that are animated with this spirit see in books

and academic work opportunities to serve a multitude of needs, including, but going beyond, the requirements of literacy and intellectual gymnastics. They use the recorded experience of mankind, as well as the present, in order to evolve a conscious way of life which all can share in common. The activities and projects of the classroom, the clubs, social events, and extracurricular activities, all are used to unite the school community together in common bonds of interest and common standards of behavior.

A careful survey of the American public school in the last fifteen years reveals significant developments in the direction just indicated. In state after state, immediately preceding the war, school people, often with the help of laymen, were in process of taking stock of their schools. From this taking of stock there emerged concrete and valuable suggestions for reorganization. State departments of education encouraged the formation of state-wide co-operative studies so that teachers in the field, with professional guidance, might gradually improve their work in harmony with the new emphasis in education: an education that centers not alone upon the intellect, but upon all phases of development relevant to living in a society diverse in character but infused with democratic ideals.

Unfortunately these promising trends in education coincided with less promising influences. The 1920's and the 1930's were difficult years for people to live through. Economic expansion with its resulting spirit of optimism in the 1920's, the expectation that we should soon be a people of assured material well-being (a chicken in every pot and two cars in each garage!) gave way to a spirit of gloom as the depression persisted.

Economic uncertainty, racial and religious antagonism resulting often in violence and the intimidation of minorities, confusion and frustration in the minds of youth, who began to feel themselves a group apart, a lost generation—all these began to generate a fear that old foundations were washing away.

It is a psychological fact that fear prompts people to revert to early patterns of behavior. The terrified adult, when confronted by a dangerous situation which he cannot resolve, tends to react as he was wont to do in childhood. So, too, of groups.

Moreover, fears do not operate singly. Fear, like misery, loves company, and human beings are peculiarly prone, when severely threatened in one area of living, to feel insecure in others. Particularly are men adept at utilizing the fears of their neighbors for the purpose of devising instruments with which to ward off threats against their own sacred preserves. Accordingly, economic conservatives see in religious instruction one means of teaching respect for traditional property rights; religious groups, fearful of the effect of science upon conventional religious ideas, and, incidentally, upon church membership, stress a necessary relationship between religious belief and adherence to the democratic form of government; political conservatives call attention to the attacks upon religion that have followed the adoption of Communism in Russia or National Socialism in Germany and use religious orthodoxy as an instrument with which to ward off both political radicalism and political liberalism.

It is not surprising, therefore, to find many serious-minded people turning to religion for an anchor to windward. Religion, as they see it, has always exercised a steadying influence on people in distress. And while not all would profess belief in what they are willing to have their children taught, they salve their consciences with the comforting observation that religion never hurt anybody. Indeed, it might render young people easier to control!

To these well-meaning adherents of programs for restoring religion to the schools we must add, for the record, both bigoted and self-styled "patriotic" groups. In predominantly Protestant communities these organizations have erected barriers to the selection of all but "Christian" teachers and, in so far as their influence can reach, have inaugurated campaigns to introduce Bible reading, daily use of the Lord's Prayer, and direct instruction in the "Christian religion" into the schools. All this with remarkably little opposition.

With what practical results? Today legislation requiring the reading of the Bible in public schools is on the increase, and pressure on behalf of religious instruction under the aegis of the school mounts daily. Moreover, where state law or constitution forbids religious instruction within the schools, provision is made for this instruction to be given on released time outside the school, often with the assistance of school authorities in the enforcement of attendance. For example, while some twelve states permit by legislative act the release of children for this purpose, in others the practice is followed without legislative sanction, indeed, in one or two instances, in defiance of an unenforced state law.

Let us turn to the arguments that religious groups advance in order to persuade the American people thus to turn back the hands upon the clock.

Chapter V

PROBABLY the most persuasive as well as the most widely accepted argument in support of religious instruction in public education derives from the popular belief that moral behavior requires a religious underpinning. According to this view, human nature cannot safely be left to its own devices, since it gravitates naturally toward evil. Only a religious faith and a regard for the consequences of transgression, as threatened by religion, can impel or compel men to follow the straight and narrow path toward righteousness.

The tendency in recent years to conceive of democracy in moral as well as political terms likewise prompts many to argue that democracy as well as morality must be grounded in conventional religion.

Here then, we are told, are two interrelated and fundamental needs of children, that schools should meet. Certainly they must educate for character, and, if democracy is to survive, they must bring up the oncoming generation so that it responds to the moral principles implicit in democracy. But to undertake this assignment and at the same time to exclude religion from the schools is to engage in an impossible undertaking. Moreover, since moral character is essential for good government, it is a matter of public concern that religion return to the schools.

To people of this conviction it is not only appropriate but essential to use the schools as an instrument for bringing religion to the unchurched as well as the churched.

Take, for example, a folder issued by the Division of Christian Education of the Protestant Council of the City of New York. This folder describes the work of the Council in connection with the released-time program of the city schools and appeals for public support with the following argument:

"What is the situation in religious literacy in New York City? There are 1,200,000 children receiving education in public, parochial, and private schools. Only 700,000 of these children are receiving any organized spiritual nurture. The remaining 500,000 children are a menace to society, to themselves, to our country and our country's future. Spiritual illiteracy must be abolished for the sake of the children and for the sake of the nation. Released time for Religious Education is the next best step we know in stamping out the spiritual illiteracy of our children." [1]

Once we concede that religious illiteracy is a public menace, the police power of the state appropriately enters the picture. It is in this vein that Erwin L. Shaver, Director of Weekday Religious Education of the International Council of Religious Education, writes with respect to a released-time program:

[1] This folder is entitled *Protestantism Unites in its Christian Education, a Practical Program of Cooperation,* and is published at 14 West 44th Street, New York 18, N.Y.

"The fifty per cent of our children who are not now receiving any training in religion because of parental neglect or other reasons should not be denied this most important element in their complete social history. When parental indifference or other circumstance has failed to give a child a healthy body, society has stepped in—by means of private or public agencies—to see that he has soundness of health. The same principle has been applied in giving every child his mental training, regardless of whether parents cared or could afford it. This has been done because the welfare of society is at stake. Social welfare is jeopardized as much or even more if any child is denied his right to know and to make use of all that society has learned in the area of religion." [2]

The arguments quoted are in support of a program of religious instruction on released time. Not all religious leaders, however, favor this specific device. They point out that it restricts religious education to verbal instruction for a limited period each week and may well impose an impossible financial strain upon the resources of church groups. Consequently it may lead to disappointment. J. Paul Williams states, for example: "There is little prospect that the public conscience of America might be so quickened that it would give, and continue year in and year out to give, the hundreds of millions of dollars which would be necessary to make the weekday program good enough to 'equal the standards of the public school.'" [3] Indeed, Williams questions whether the funds required to put weekday religious schools on an

2 "The Weekday Church School—Opportunity and Challenge." *Information Service,* Department of Research and Education, Federal Council of Churches of Christ in America, XXI, No. 22 (May 29, 1943).

3 *The New Education and Religion.* New York: Association Press, 1945, p. 125.

adequate footing might not better be used to improve the Sunday school "and provide for a full half day in the Sunday school."

Dissatisfaction with the potentialities of released-time programs for character building lead to two practical suggestions: one, that provision be made for religious instruction within the school; and, two, that public support be extended to parochial schools.

In communities predominantly of one faith, energetic efforts are made to bring about direct teaching of non-sectarian religion within the schools. Thus the Superintendent of Schools of Atlanta, Georgia, insists that

"basically, religion is concerned with two fundamental ideas or experiences; first, man's relationship to God, and second, his relationship to the universe about him, including his fellowmen. . . . We can help each youth of the nation to become aware that there is something bigger than himself. . . . When the schools have taught this fundamental idea of the existence of God, of a Supreme Being who, in the definition of the multitudes, is omnipotent, omniscient, all-merciful, all-loving, and just, who presides over the destinies of men, they have given a firm anchorage to youth." [4]

And a publication of the National Reform Association, entitled *God in Our Public Schools,* goes so far as to argue that the Supreme Court of the United States has held that this country is a Christian nation. This having been established by our highest legal authority, it follows that the teaching of Christianity in our schools is not sectarian. Sectarian doctrines are merely those upon

[4] Quoted by J. Paul Williams, *op. cit.,* p. 143.

which Christian sects disagree. Consequently, objections to the teaching of Christianity in our schools are without legal foundation! "No," exclaims the author, "Uncle Sam is not an atheist, nor a secularist, but a Christian. Sad to say, he has adopted some pagan practices and must get right with God by restoring religion to the schools or perish through secularism and crime." [5]

Groups more disposed to follow a policy of live and let live suggest that public schools engage teachers with an eye to a one-to-one comparison between the faiths of pupils and the faiths of teachers. This would enable the school to divide pupils into religious classes on sectarian lines and insure the instruction of children by teachers of an appropriate faith. Advocates of this plan consider it superior to released time, since it would be financed by the state and would make possible the more frequent meeting of classes in religion than on a released-time program and, consequently, more intensive instruction. It would also insure both the supervision of instruction and the maintenance of standards by public-school authorities.

Of this plan Williams remarks:

"It would probably be much easier than most people suppose to get public support for this scheme. If it were seriously proposed by some governmental or ecclesiastical body, a storm of protest would immediately follow. But the leaders of the larger denominations of the nation might quickly see that this plan preserves the religious liberty of the sect and provides for more adequate religious instruction. If the sec-

[5] W. S. Fleming, *God in Our Public Schools*. Pittsburgh, Pa.: National Reform Association, 1944, pp. 111–112.

tarian leaders did come to see this and united in advocating such a plan it would surely carry the nation. Our religious leaders have no one to blame but themselves for the deplorable state of religious education; for the political potency of the united religious forces of the country is overwhelming. Archbishop Ireland phrased the situation neatly when he said: 'In our fear lest Protestants gain some advantage over Catholics or Catholics over Protestants, we have given over our schools to unbelievers and secularists.' " [6]

The conviction that morality stems directly from religion leads to a revival of the ancient principle of state aid to parochial schools. Until a few years ago the friends of state subsidies to parochial schools were confined almost exclusively to Catholics. Educators generally did not approve of it, since they recalled the way in which, in the nineteenth century, state-supported private schools bitterly opposed and often succeeded in retarding the development of public schools. In New York State, for example, where private academies had long fed upon public monies, the development of public high schools was retarded by at least a generation.

Catholics, however, have never reconciled themselves to the theory that education is a state function, in the sense that the state should itself provide education, particularly when this education is either nonsectarian or secular in character. This view was forcefully stated a few years ago by George Johnson, formerly Educational Director of the National Catholic Welfare Conference,

[6] *Op. cit.*, p. 147. For a Catholic argument in favor of this plan see A. J. Talley's "The Religion of Our Youth," *Proceedings of the National Catechetical Congress of the Confraternity of Christian Doctrine.* Paterson, N.J.: St. Anthony Guild Press, 1937, p. 82.

in an article written for the *Atlantic Monthly*. Johnson contends:

"To attempt to make children and youth conformable to the image of the Savior by means of some occasional religious instruction and then teach them the arts and sciences in conformity with the spirit of the world is to court failure. It suggests to the impressionable mind of the child that religion does not really matter in the same way that other things matter. He does not see it entering into the warp and woof of life and unless a man's religion does enter into the warp and woof of life it has little more than emotional or pietistic value.

"In the Catholic school, religion is not regarded as just one branch in the curriculum. It is not confined to mere religious instruction. It is the foundation, the heart and soul of all other disciplines." [7]

Johnson might have added that since, in Catholic theory, the Church possesses infallibility, it ranks first in the hierarchy of education. As Redden and Ryan insist in a recent volume,[8] the concerns of the Church extend to every human activity. It can, indeed it must, "advise and command parents about the form, organization and content of the school to which their children should be sent," and it "is ever mindful of the legitimate rights and duties of the family and the State," in no way interfering, of course, "with these rights and duties when each society properly discharges them." But since "God granted His Church infallibility," there is no objective

[7] "The Catholic Schools in America," *Atlantic Monthly*, CLXV (April, 1940), p. 500.
[8] *Freedom Through Education*. Milwaukee, Wisconsin: Bruce Publishing Co., 1944.

appeal from the injunctions of the Church in the event of conflict.

J. Paul Williams contends that one weakness in Protestant religious education has been its reliance upon an exclusively verbal instruction in contrast with a thoroughgoing induction into a way of life such as characterizes Catholic education.

Now if we relate the fact that sound instruction in religion requires more than occasional classroom instruction of a verbal character, to the belief that religion is indispensable for character education, we give plausibility to an appeal for state support of private religious schools. This is the basis upon which Williams is moved to argue for governmental support of sectarian schools. As he sees it:

"We live in a day when the functions of government are being greatly increased; this increase is in general salutary, for individual initiative has shown its weakness in many areas. The three questions which should be asked about any extension of public responsibility are: 1. Is the proposed activity essential to public welfare? 2. Is private enterprise adequately meeting the need? 3. If private enterprise is not meeting the need, is it reasonable to suppose that by any means it can be brought to meet the need? If the propositions which have been stated on previous pages concerning present religious education are accepted, it is obvious that adequate provision for education in religion is an activity essential to public welfare, and that private enterprise is not only not meeting the need but is not likely to meet it. Thus some type of public support for religious education would seem to be essential." [9]

[9] *Op. cit.,* p. 130.

In justice to Williams it must be said that he foresees serious objections to the immediate adoption of a plan for public support of sectarian schools. He recognizes that it would destroy the unity of the American people and run counter to widespread loyalty to the public school. Consequently he limits himself, for the present, to a plea for more general support of parochial schools, Catholic and non-Catholic, and for the concentration of effort upon the gradual infiltration of religious instruction into the public schools along lines already mentioned.[10] Others, however, are impatient of delay. Much of the support now given to plans for Federal aid to "non-public" as well as to public education derives from the fact that an increasing number of people are no longer sensitive, as they once were, to the dangers in a policy of state assistance to parochial schools.

II

A second argument on behalf of bringing religion into the school emphasizes the failure of the home and the church to minister adequately to this important phase of development. Consequently, religious leaders look hopefully to the school.

Here motives are mixed, with two predominating. The

---

[10] A careful reading of Williams's book leaves one somewhat confused. Evidently he is friendly to different solutions of the problem of religious education, as circumstances dictate. Education in sectarian schools alone meets his criteria for religious education. This being out of the question at present, he endorses a series of procedures: increased private support of parochial schools, religious instruction by teachers of pupils of different faiths in the public schools at public expense, and even a watered-down program of a practical character in which to the teaching of knowledge about religion in the schools there is added instruction in democracy as a religion.

first is practical and mundane in its objectives; the second, earnest and sincere in its concern for the child's orientation in a genuinely religious experience. Let us begin with the second.

This conceives of the school as essentially the last bulwark of a thoroughgoing religious education. It stems from the findings of psychologists and educators, who demonstrate conclusively that any education worth its salt must go beyond verbal presentation and verbal assent. Education, these experts insist, is a process in which an individual continuously reconstructs and reorganizes his personality—thought, feeling, and behavior —in the actual give and take of living. Out of vital experiences emerge ideals which modify subsequent behavior; and, on the other hand, behavior that is meaningful inevitably influences ideals. Thus conceived, religious education requires both an environment in which children can practice what is preached and an instruction that encourages them to formulate their own ideals in harmony with a religious way of life.

Obviously few institutions in contemporary society succeed in affording young people a religious education of this character. As J. Paul Williams indicates, Sunday schools, vacation schools, and education on a released-time basis, in co-operation with public schools, all suffer in contrast with education in an all-day school. Effective religious education, he contends, must use the environment to reach and employ the emotions and the will as well as the intellect. "If the high aims of religious education are to be achieved a great deal more skill must be developed on the part of religious teachers, much more time must be spent in religious instruction, the school must operate in a superior physical plant." [11]

Indeed, when measured against these standards, only an occasional home succeeds in combining precept and example with opportunities for consistent practice sufficient to meet the religious needs of children. It is natural, therefore, for F. Ernest Johnson to insist that the school should supplement the home. As he sees it:

"It is the function of the school to rise above the cultural level of the home *as is*. The school is a selective instrumentality with reference to the culture. We expect it to lift the level of the common life. The average American home is no more in a position to carry responsibility for the religious education of children and youth than it is to conduct their public education." [12]

Both Williams and Johnson conclude from the obvious failure of institutions and instrumentalities other than the school that public education can no longer safely ignore the religious needs of young people.

Before we develop the implications of these conclusions, let us turn to the more mundane arguments on behalf of introducing religious education into public schools. These worldly motives originate in the fear that unless the schools are thus used, the churches will shortly lack public support and will dwindle in enrollment and power.

For example, no more than 43 per cent of the population of the United States are members of churches,

[11] *Op. cit.,* p. 113.
[12] *The Social Gospel Re-examined.* New York: Harper & Brothers, 1940, pp. 179–180.

and a steadily increasing number of children are untouched by the churches. As Professor Conrad H. Moehlman indicates in this connection:

"In 1936 the five-to-seventeen-age population in the United States was 31,618,000. The total Sunday school enrollment was less than five million. About 57 per cent of the Catholic five-to-seventeen-year-old children were not in parochial schools. In Protestant parochial schools the total enrollment was only 275,643. Between 1926 and 1936, Sunday school enrollment decreased forty per cent. In that year the United States Baptists had over three million less Sunday school pupils than church members." [13]

Moehlman also draws attention to the fact that Americans are steadily losing interest in the "older forms, expressions, and postulates of religion." As evidence he refers to a survey of American life conducted some years ago and recorded in *Recent Social Trends*.[14] This survey indicates that in 1900 the number of subscriptions to Protestant religious periodicals exceeded subscriptions to popular scientific magazines by four and one-half times, but in 1930 the proportions were exactly reversed. "In the magazines for American intellectuals, interest in the ethical aspects of religion increased; interest in the dogmas of Christianity decreased. Interest in traditional Christian emphases between 1905 and 1930 (an infallible Bible, traditional creeds, church organization, denominational propaganda) declined fifty per cent, but in-

[13] *School and Church, the American Way*. New York and London: Harper & Brothers, 1944, p. 123.
[14] *Recent Social Trends in the United States;* Report of the President's Research Committee on Social Trends. New York: McGraw-Hill Book Co., 1933.

terest in open-minded religion (prayer, worship, spiritual life, social problems) improved." [15]

These trends do not depress Moehlman. On the contrary, he concludes that the Christian virtues of "tolerance, sympathetic understanding, religious idealism" are as vital as ever. They indicate merely that the sources of inspiration in American life are not predominantly in the churches. Moreover, he contends that "for all Americans the postulates of the democratic way are also sincere religious convictions."

This shift from the churches to other sources of inspiration for the good life is less satisfactory to men and women whose concern it is to perpetuate and expand time-honored institutions of religion. They see in the schools an instrument admirably designed to increase interest and, through interest, enrollments in the churches. For example, W. Dyer Blair states in the *Church Monthly* of the Riverside Church, New York City, for May 1940: "Neither the Sunday school, the vacation church school, nor the young people's societies, nor all these combined, reach as high a percentage of the total youth group in a great many communities as does the weekday school." According to Blair the plan of releasing pupils from school during the school day, in order that they may attend church schools, results in an enrollment of 90 to 99 per cent of the public school constituency in many localities. And this in turn, it is hoped, will eventually swell the rosters of the churches.

Obviously, the more energetic the co-operative spirit

[15] *Op. cit.,* p. 125.

of the public school, the higher will this percentage rise. Consequently, the introduction of religious instruction into the schools is but the first step in a more far-reaching program.

In New York City, for example, the regulations of the Board of Education endeavor to place primary responsibility for registration and attendance of children upon the home and the church school. In theory, it is not the function of the public school to bring about the child's initial registration in the church school nor to discipline him for failure to attend these classes. In practice, however, as revealed in a study of the released-time program by the Public Education Association, many teachers and principals of conviction violate these instructions, in part because of loyalty to the church of their own affiliation, and in part because, as conscientious officials, they cannot countenance carelessness and irregularity in attendance on the part of children.

Nor are all communities as scrupulous as New York City in its relations with church schools. Once boards of education sanction religious instruction on school time, school officials tend to assume a responsibility for enforcing enrollment as well as attendance. The result is, of course, that public schools become in effect recruiting centers for the sectarian affiliation of children. Church leaders justify this fact on the ground that it brings children of the unchurched into the fold and decreases the spiritual illiteracy of our population. As Erwin L. Shaver puts it: "Wherever a *co-operative* weekday church school has been in operation, it has succeeded in reaching on the average one third of this neglected half of our children and youth, a remarkable evangelistic record." [16]

III

In recent years the campaign to bring religion back to the schools has received the vigorous support of a group of religious liberals, who challenge the place of the secular school in American life as well as an interpretation of the principle of separation of church and state which leads to the exclusion of religious instruction from public education. They likewise question traditional and conventional notions of the term religion.

This group begins by stressing the fact that it is sectarianism and not religion which the law excludes from the public schools. Sectarian rivalry was admittedly an evil. William Clayton Bower writes, for example, that "as long as religion was thought of in terms of sectarian theology and ecclesiasticism the problem of the relation of religion to education in a democracy was insoluble in any terms other than the exclusion of religion from general education." [17] Today, however, this exclusion would seem to be unnecessary since we conceive of education and religion in different terms.

The identification of religion with sectarianism, it is held, leads to false conclusions regarding the prohibitions commonly found in state constitutions and legislative acts. F. Ernest Johnson quotes a state superintendent of public instruction who remarks that "under our law, no religious instruction can be given," whereas the

[16] *Op. cit.*
[17] *Church and State in Education.* Chicago: University of Chicago Press, 1944, p. 6.

section of the law upon which the superintendent based his position merely reads: "No sectarian doctrine may be taught or inculcated in any of the public schools of the state." [18]

A mistaken identification of sectarianism and religion has led to unfortunate results in American education and American life. It coincided with the period in which our people began successfully to exploit the material resources of the continent and in the process fell victims "to material scales of value." Moreover, it is charged, our secular schools have failed to offset and correct a shallowness in contemporary American culture. Rather have they contributed often to a false sense of values. Accordingly, in seeking to restore religion to education we are, in fact, bringing somewhat belatedly into the schools principles that may lead to the spiritual integration of our culture.

What are the characteristics of religion and a religious education that contrast with instruction in sectarian doctrine?

It is at this point that a knowledge of semantics may help the reader, since the argument turns upon transformations in the term religion. Take, for example, the argument advanced by William Clayton Bower in his little volume entitled *Church and State in Education*.[19] According to Bower, new definitions of education, religion, and the national community call for a new division of responsibility between church and state. Edu-

[18] *Information Service*. Department of Research and Education, Federal Council of Churches of Christ in America. XIX, No. 43 (December 28, 1940).
[19] *Op. cit.*

cation he conceives in progressive terms. The old education was formal, external, and authoritative, concerned with transmitting knowledge and information as something externally formulated. The new education takes its cue from a creative interrelationship between the individual and the "objective world of nature, society and culture." Attention thus shifts from "teaching to learning and from passive assimilation of tradition to inquiry, commitment and constructive action." Under these conditions the process of education "overruns the boundaries of any given institution, be it the school, the family, or the church"; and to ignore the values and ideals with which young people are to shape their lives is impossible.

So, too, with the nature of religion. Viewed structurally, this is sectarian and cannot be tolerated in the public school. But religion is no longer conceived in terms of theology, ceremonial, and ecclesiastical institutions. Scientific, historical, and psychological studies reveal it to be a function of living, "a phase of people's total culture." Thus conceived, it attains expression in different forms in different times and cultures, even in different cultural areas within the nation. As a "people's total interaction with the objective world of nature, organized society, and the accumulated traditions of the historic past," it serves a twofold and reciprocal function. It appears as a value that revalues, interprets, and integrates all other values and, in so doing, it "reacts upon each particular interest and activity as a factor of reconstruction." Thus does it offset the divisive influence of specialization peculiar to advanced societies.

It is religion, then, that breathes a necessary unity into our national life. And in one of its functions, it is the purpose of religion both to create and to give expression to a people's idealism. Bower contends that as a people we have reached a stage of development in which states that were once isolated have attained the status of a national community under a government that is more than a system of checks and balances. Government also strives to give positive expression to measures that serve the people's needs. As such, church and state complement each other. Only on a structural or institutional level do they compete. "As creatures of the comprehending community, both serve the needs of the community and are answerable to it. . . . These needs of the whole people are interrelated needs that cannot be separated from the living tissue of interaction that is the American community." Nor can religious needs be separated from other needs, since each—intellectual, economic, political, aesthetic, and moral—is necessarily set "in the context of man's relation to the whole of reality and lifted to a conscious level of responsibility to God as the ground of that reality." [20]

Bower, in common with F. Ernest Johnson, J. Paul Williams, and others, insists that it is misleading to identify religion with any one specific content of belief, except in so far as content involves common elements; and by common element is evidently meant not an arbitrary item of belief or of creed, but rather an attitude. As Johnson states, it is not something that has to do

[20] Bower, *op. cit.*, pp. 53–56.

"with doctrinal statements of what *is* but with those assumptions concerning the good life which hold society together; with belief in the value of reverence, in the importance of belonging to a worshipping, working religious community; with devotion to ends that find their meaning outside the scope and span of the individual life—in short if what is meant is acceptance of spiritual values that make for the unity of a dynamic culture, should we then say that education is not directly concerned in fostering and enriching such religious faith?" [21]

Williams has something similar in mind when he insists that "Our society will consider religious education of fundamental importance when educators come to think of religious education as the process, wherever it is conducted, of helping society to decide what is the chief end of communal living." [22]

All this is fairly clear until we read in Williams that the process which helps men to decide "the chief end of communal living" is identical with "what a person (or a group) does to keep moving in line with what the person (or group) believes to be the fundamental demands which the universe makes on human beings."

Careful readers will observe at this point that the "process" or the "function" of religion which Americans must bring into the school begins to bear a close resemblance to its "structure."

So too with Bower. He begins, as we have seen, by separating religion as a function from religion as a structure and then proceeds to add small bits of content

[21] *Information Service,* XIX, No. 43 (December 28, 1940).
[22] *Op. cit.,* p. 16.

until religion is clothed pretty much in conventional garb. In its naked state, functional religion is the "valuation process," the attempt to read unity and direction in life by means of ideals. As such it is, of course, common to men in all cultures, although the answers thus given to life's problems vary widely as we move from culture to culture. Very shortly, however, this function takes on more ambitious proportions. It becomes a process by means of which each value is "brought under the judgment of all other values" and "is appraised in the searching light of fundamental and comprehending values which the religious mind associates with God." Somewhat later this, too, is identified with the idea of "the brotherhood of man and the fatherhood of God." By this time the meat upon the bones of religion as a "function" is sufficient to stir the blood of the hounds of sectarianism!

Having distinguished to their satisfaction religion as a function from religion as a structure, our authors indicate six ways in which functional religion may be included in the program of the schools:

1. The schools can and should convey to young people knowledge about religion. In this contention Bower is ably seconded by both F. Ernest Johnson and J. Paul Williams. For example, Johnson writes:

"The schools should include in the social studies, precisely as they include other aspects of community organization, the institutions of organized religion. Religion, like law, politics, economics, is a kind of *activity* which has always had its most significant expression in institutional forms." [23]

[23] *Information Service*, XXII, No. 1, Part I (Jan. 2, 1943).

And Williams, while admitting that knowledge does not in itself insure wise living, believes that "if Americans generally could come to have a greater knowledge of religion, the result would be a genuine improvement in the religious quality of American life. Knowledge is power; it is one of the tools of maturity." [24]

Williams also believes that greater knowledge of religion, conveyed through the schools, "would decrease the religious prejudice of the American people," diminish the ignorance of religion which is characteristic of the younger generation of today, and, by sharing the task of teaching religious information with sectarian schools, would raise the standard of performance in the latter. "A division of labor would be established between these two types of school. The sectarian school would be in a position to build on the foundation laid by the public schools, and the public schools would studiously avoid making any sectarian appeal. Public school teaching would thus be objective in the sense that it would present all the major religious systems." [25]

2. Schools and colleges can include religion as "a field of knowledge comparable with the fields of literature, natural science, history, philosophy, the social sciences, and the arts." [26] Likewise, on the lower levels of education, religion becomes a legitimate object of study, in order that young people may come to know the religious roots of their culture.[27]

3. The school can cultivate religious attitudes by

24 *Op. cit.*, p. 176.
25 *Ibid.*, pp. 178–179.
26 Bower, *op. cit.*, p. 63.
27 Johnson, *op. cit.* (Jan. 2, 1943).

utilizing ceremonials and celebrations in connection with seasonal events such as Thanksgiving, Christmas, New Year's, and Easter. They can likewise foster understanding and appreciation as between the great religious faiths—Protestant, Catholic, and Jewish—by using classical symbols and celebrations peculiar to these faiths. "The school, as the one common meeting place of all the component elements in the community, offers an universally favorable opportunity for such a common sharing of the attitudes and ideals of the various groups that constitute its common life." [28]

4. Actual participation in the life of the school and the community can give "the growing person an actual experience of the higher spiritual values involved" in these relationships. Bower calls attention to ten categories of values, "that are basically religious," which Dr. Ernest J. Chave observed to be operative within the work of an elementary school. These are:

"A sense of the worth of persons, developing social sensitivity, growth in appreciation of the universe, growth in the discrimination of values, growth in the sense of responsibility and accountability, recognition of the need for co-operative fellowship, recognition that the quest for truth and the realization of ideals is a slow and endless pursuit, development of a working philosophy of life, observance of special times and ceremonies, and development of adequate means of expression of spiritual values and ideals." [29]

5. The school can explore the "possibilities of religion as a principle of the integration of education and the

28 Bower, *op. cit.*, p. 68.
29 *Ibid.*, p. 66.

culture." According to Bower religion has as one of its functions the task of revaluing interests and activities so as "to unite them into a total meaning and worth of life in terms of its responsible relation to God. Its other function is to subject every practical interest and activity of the common life to cross-examination and reconstruction in the light of this core of fundamental values." [30]

6. Finally, the schools can use religion in the person-to-person relationships of teacher and student. As Johnson puts it:

"With no end of respect for psychiatrists, I nevertheless believe—and I think the more profound of them recognize—that a sense of guilt is more often genuine than phony. And the only right way to get rid of such a sense of guilt is to remove the guilt. In this exploitive world the absence of a sense of guilt is often the most ominous sign a personality can show.

"Undoubtedly, a morbid religious consciousness has disordered many a life. But a healthy religious faith and discipline is a powerful organizing force. . . . One of our greatest educational needs is to explore the resources of religion in personal counseling." [31]

I shall return in the next chapter to this discussion of the nature of religion.

Four major considerations thus impel people today to advocate restoring religion to the public school, even at the cost of repudiating the time-honored principle of separation of church and state. First is the popular no-

[30] *Ibid.*, p. 70.
[31] Johnson, *op. cit.* (Jan. 2, 1943).

tion that moral behavior and, consequently, character development run counter to normal tendencies in human nature; that right action naturally kicks against the pricks. Accordingly, when citizens observe an alarming increase in juvenile delinquency and crime and are told quite properly that schools must educate for character, they are prone to turn to religious instruction as a means of salvation. From this other conclusions follow. Erasing religious illiteracy assumes the aspect of a public health measure, even though to do so involves putting pressure on the unchurched as well as the churched. On this assumption, too, contributions from the public purse in support of parochial education are sanctioned, if they are needed.

Second, both the nature of sound education, as psychologists and modern educators conceive it, and conditions of spiritual undernourishment in a majority of homes, are thought to require a revision of the traditional formula regulating relations between school and church. An education designed to influence character must go deeper than is permitted by experiences confined to the printed page or to mere talk in the classroom. In order to become directive forces in an individual's life, ideals and ideas require both outlets for action and opportunities to control action. The school must, therefore, concern itself with the whole child; and no child can become whole without instruction in religion.

Third, there are administrative and institutional reasons that prompt the organized forces of religion to turn to the school at this time. Membership in the churches is on the decline. Enrollments in parochial schools and

Sunday schools alike are decreasing ominously. The public school holds forth alluring possibilities as a potential recruiting agency for the churches.

Finally, a reinterpretation of the term and the concept of religion prompts liberals in theology to urge a revision in the accepted functions of the school. These liberals insist that religion and sectarianism are in no way identical; that religion is nothing other than man's attempt to evolve values as directive influences out of the stream of life and to appraise conduct in terms of these standards and values. So conceived, all men are religious and no education is possible without religion. Sectarianism, on the other hand, pertains to the creeds that divide people one from the other. Banish sectarianism, by all means, these men cry, but provide a central and controlling place in our schools for religion, lest the salt of education lose its flavor.

With the case for the intervention of religion in public education before us, let us turn to opposing considerations.

Chapter VI

CAN OUR PUBLIC SCHOOLS DEVELOP SOUND MORALITY WITHOUT INSTRUCTION IN RELIGION?

SEVERAL years ago Dr. Joseph J. Reilly of Hunter College, New York City, delivered a series of radio addresses entitled "God and American Education." In one of these he warned his hearers against the influence of John Dewey and William Kilpatrick, arguing that they promote a naturalistic morality, a morality that finds its source and its justification within the nature of man and his relations with his fellows, rather than in revealed religion. This view is dangerous, Dr. Reilly contends, since it leaves morality rudderless and also puts democracy in the place of religion. Democracy, he holds,

"derives its reason for being, its life, its vitality, its spiritual force, solely from religion, because the freedom and the rights that constitute democracy have their origin only in God from whom they come as free gifts to man. . . .

"The democratic conception of the dignity of the human being, the worth of human personality, has its foundation in religion. Religion teaches that man is the handiwork of the Creator, that we are individually his children and made to his image and likeness."

Dr. Reilly gives expression in these remarks to a view widely held: that morality and democracy—that is, the moral principles implicit in the democratic way of life —can be taught effectively in the schools only when they are grounded explicitly in religion. From this it follows that the "godless" school cannot be tolerated. And by a "godless" school critics of public education mean the secular school, since it fails to provide specifically for religious instruction.

Often the charge is made that juvenile delinquency results from the omission of religious influences in the lives of children and can be checked only by bringing religion back to the school. As one advocate of a released-time program in New York expressed it some years ago in a letter to *The New York Times*.

"A good Catholic can never be a bad citizen. Likewise, neither can a good Protestant or a good Jew fail in his civic or moral obligation. If, as one authority has said, there are hundreds of thousands of 'spiritually hungry and spiritually naked' children in New York City alone, then a challenge exists that must be met promptly and fully. These children, to be good citizens, are in desperate need of religious orientation."

The assumption that morality hinges on religious instruction leads easily to the conclusion that unless the state fosters religious education public health will suffer. Indeed, as we saw in the last chapter, religious interests are now demanding on precisely these grounds the intervention of the state in order to remedy religious illiteracy.

It is therefore highly important to examine the assumption that both sound morality and democracy are rooted exclusively in religion.

Support for this theory is not confined to the popular

mind. In 1942 seven professors at Princeton University issued a statement entitled "The Spiritual Basis of Democracy." In this they contend that "democratic institutions and cultural activities rest on the assumption that man, while a part of nature, is a spiritual being and that his highest good should be defined in terms of spiritual values. The major problem which confronts us at this time, therefore, is not merely the defense of democracy and its culture, but a deeper understanding of and commitment to the spiritual conception of man upon which democracy is based."

Now by spiritual these professors do not mean merely man's highest nature as commonly conceived, the ideals and aspirations that he evolves and creates out of experience with life. Rather do they mean something other-worldly, something, as they themselves say, that is identifiable "only by means of distinctive methods and categories suitable to its distinctive nature" and (as it follows, of course) revealed to us by an authority other than reason and judgment and the ordinary rules of evidence.

Possession of this spiritual nature enables man to transcend his animal limitations and to relate himself to ideal reality that is super-individual. From this reality man derives his morality, and since morality is basic to democracy, and democracy is "meaningless without the kind of moral responsibility which spiritual beings alone acknowledge," it follows that democracy, like morality, is grounded exclusively on this spiritual conception of life.

Observe that we said "*this* spiritual conception of life"; for it is central to the argument that democracy is correctly grounded only in one spiritual conception of life. To be sure, our professors draw attention to two possible conceptions in which we may root democracy, the contemplative-mystical conception that derives from the Greeks, and the Hebrew-Christian conception. From a brief review of these two they conclude, however, that the second alone, the Hebrew-Christian, is valid, although both are superior to the modern naturalistic view, "which exalts man as such and by himself." Naturalism, according to our authors, "leads inevitably to pride and egoism," and unless identified for what it is will lead to the destruction of democracy. "If scholars, teachers, writers and religious leaders do not succeed," they exclaim, "in arousing the minds and hearts of the democratic peoples to a living faith in the spiritual nature of man" (but, observe, spiritual as defined above) "the direct defense of democracy by military and political action is bound to fail. It is not primarily two different forms of government but two different conceptions of human life which are opposed in the life and death struggle of today."

Here we have boldly stated the argument of one influential section of public opinion in support of the inclusion of religion in education. Evidently democracy and morality both depend not merely upon religion, but upon the one valid religion, the Hebrew-Christian! Taken literally this means that a democratic association of the nations of the world must wait upon the conversion of all peoples to a religion that stems solely from the Hebrew-Christian tradition. Which is another way of asserting that international morality and the forms of government to which it will give rise in the future must rest upon a common culture rather than upon a plurality of cultures.

Thus stated, the merging of religion and public education is indeed of supreme importance. If the argument summarized is sound, our schools should incorporate, and without delay, the true religion within their curricula. But suppose the contention be false? Then we are equally obliged to identify it as one more attempt to further the interests of a sectarian conception of life at the expense of other conceptions.

II

Let us consider first the argument that religion underwrites democracy.

Few will deny that the Hebrew prophets contributed liberally to the evolution of democracy. Not only did they assert boldly the rights of the humblest members of the community, if need be against the king himself, but in subordinating the interests of all men irrespective of worldly position and power to an overarching concept of justice, they gave to mankind a criterion with which continuously to examine and appraise the social, economic, and political order. Likewise the democratic concept of the worth of the individual finds expression in the utterances of the prophets of Israel and in the rugged independence of mind they fostered. Not without avail did they promote the idea that in the sight of God the slave is the equal of the mightiest prince.

But this is only half the picture. The Hebrew ideal of government was a theocracy, not a democracy, and even the concept of social democracy occasionally pictured in the Bible remained far more an ideal than a reality. Let us not forget that the reformer and the fanatic defender of the *status quo* alike have drawn their inspiration and authority from the Bible. Did not the churches of this country, less than a century ago, divide on the issue of slavery, and did not each faction quote from the same Bible in support of its position? How often have the pronouncements of St. Paul been used to enjoin men to submit to the "powers that be" no matter how oppressive since, as "God's ministers," they are to be endured and obeyed!

Nor can we use the early Christian communistic communities as illustrations of genuinely democratic living. The fact is that democracy, as we envisage it today, derives from plural sources: in part from Hebrew and Christian, in part from the Greeks; in large measure from the philosophy of the Stoics and from the Roman law which gave expression to Stoic principles; from economic developments in Europe since the fifteenth century; from the fearless methods of thinking developed by modern science; and, in no small degree, from the relations of man to man which were peculiar to life on the frontier.

No, the facts of history do not sustain the view that the principles of democracy require the acceptance of a religious conception of life. We might add, with Sidney Hook,[1] that logic also fails to sustain this contention. As Hook points out:

[1] See "The New Failure of Nerve," *Partisan Review*, X (January–February, 1943), pp. 2–23; also "The Philosophical Presupposition of Democracy," *Ethics*, LII (April, 1942), pp. 275–296.

"From the alleged fact that all men are equal before God, it does not follow logically that they are, or should be, equal before the state or enjoy equal rights in the community. This must be justified by other considerations. Even on the theological scheme, although God is equally the creator of angels, men, animals and things, they are not all equal in value before him." [2]

And, forsooth, is it not a cardinal principle of democracy that a man is a man for "a' that," irrespective of origin, and thereby is entitled to equal and open opportunity for the development of his potentialities?

As a matter of fact, men have used religion to justify both equality and inequality. As Hook states,

"Some Christians have held—with as much logic as their brethren who draw contrary conclusions—that because all men are equally sinners in the sight of the Lord, their social and political inequalities in this transitory life are unimportant." [3]

It seems that neither logic nor history can sustain the assertion that religion, or one brand of religion in particular, underwrites democracy. Moreover, it is highly important to recognize that the potential sources of democracy are plural. To inculcate a parochial conception in the minds of young people on the eve of a second attempt to develop an organization of the nations of the world is both shortsighted and dangerous. Arrogant assertions of superiority in race and religion belong to the past, not to the future. In contrast, world reconstruction requires a genuine humbleness of spirit, a willing-

[2] *Partisan Review*, X, p. 21.
[3] *Ibid.*, p. 21.

ness to welcome and to utilize where possible the contributions from many cultures and to weave these contributions into new and suggestive patterns for living.

Several years ago Lawrence K. Frank developed a fruitful point of view in an article entitled "World Order and Cultural Diversity." [4] In this article Frank points out that despite all "differences in size, shape, color and in some physiological functions, man as a species is essentially alike everywhere." Everywhere also man encounters what Frank calls persistent tasks of life, problems associated with the gaining of food, clothing, shelter, security, with organizing group life and regulating human conduct by transforming impulsive behavior into standards and codes and methods of living cherished by a group. In seeking to realize these ends he evolves assumptions about himself, about nature and the world. Out of these assumptions grow his religion, his philosophy, his art, and his social, economic, and political institutions. Now, as we examine these varying philosophies, religions, and practices, we discover certain valuable insights into man's nature and his needs; and we observe also that no one cultural expression is complete or adequate in itself. Each is limited, partial, and can with profit be supplemented by the insights of others.

Accordingly, it is not enough to familiarize young people with the values of their own culture—important as this may be. Their education should include as well an acquaintance with, imbued with a respect for, the convictions and the practices of other times and places. By comparison and contrast they will be encouraged to

[4] *Free World,* June, 1942.

hold fast to the things that are good in their inheritance and to improve on this inheritance at points where change seems advisable.

III

There seems to be no occasion for believing that schools must include instruction in religion in order to insure a loyalty to the principles of democracy. But what of the contention that morality is rudderless without religious sanction, and that schools cannot safely abstain from religious education if they would develop sound character?

Fortunately we are not restricted entirely to a theoretical discussion of this problem. Careful investigations into the relation of church membership to crime and into the effects of instruction in religion upon delinquency bear directly upon these claims.

An excellent summary of studies in this area is contained in an address delivered several years ago by Dr. Negley K. Teeters before the Conference on the Scientific Spirit and the Democratic Faith.[5] According to Dr. Teeters the results of investigation run counter to popular conviction. For example, take the religious affiliations of inmates of prisons. Dr. Teeters shows that in a group of twenty-seven penitentiaries and nineteen reform schools 71.8 per cent of the inmates were affiliated with some religion, whereas only 46.6 per cent of the total population in the United States are members

[5] This address was delivered at the Society for Ethical Culture, New York City, on May 29, 1943. It was entitled "The Role of Religious Education in Delinquency and Crime," and was reprinted in *The Arbitrator* of July–August, 1943.

of religious bodies. Similarly from a study conducted by Franklin Steiner on the religious preferences of prison inmates, it was found that of 85,000 individuals 80 per cent expressed a preference for Christianity; only 8,000 indicated no preference at all, and a mere 150 identified themselves as either atheists or agnostics!

Investigations into the relation of education and criminality are equally interesting. For example, Dr. Frank L. Christian, onetime superintendent of Elmira Reformatory, reports that of 22,000 inmates only four were college graduates. As Teeters remarks, "Not all lists would run as low as this as we find in more recent years more white collar criminals running afoul of the law. But it is still equally true that the highly educated classes rarely find their way into prison."

But what of the religious instruction of children? Probably the most extensive study of this character was conducted some years ago by Hugh Hartshorne and Mark May and published in a three-volume work under the general title, *Studies in the Nature of Character.* The investigators found, from an exhaustive comparison of the actions of children under stress, that those who attended Sunday schools acted no better than did children of similar background who lacked religious instruction. Indeed the authors conclude that "apparently, the tendency to deceive is about as prevalent among those enrolled in Sunday school as it is among those who are not."

Dr. George Rex Mursall of the Ohio Department of Welfare arrived at similar conclusions from a comparison of a group of boys in the Ohio Reform School at Lancaster with law-abiding children outside. This investigation indicated that the inmates of the reformatory had received fully as much religious training as had non-offenders. Mursall concluded from the evidence that "it seems safe to state that there is no significant relation between religious training and delinquent or non-delinquent behavior."

Finally Teeters cites the study of Professor Hightower of the University of Iowa. Professor Hightower tested 3,000 children for lying, cheating, and deception. His results forced the conclusion that "there appears to be no relationship of any consequence between Biblical information and the different phases of conduct studied . . . It indicates very definitely that mere knowledge of the Bible is not in itself sufficient to insure character growth."

What moral do we draw from these data? Not that we should refrain from introducing young people to their religious heritage. This introduction can be justified on grounds quite different from those examined. Two conclusions, however, do follow: First, faith without works is dead. Verbal instruction carries no assurance in itself that conduct will eventuate in harmony with precepts taught. Only when the day-by-day life in the school, the home, the community, gives body and substance to what is taught and, conversely, when abundant occasion is found for precept to control practice, will instruction influence the springs of conduct. Second, the data suggest that both the ideas and the activities which create character have their roots in experiences that transcend the theological and religious affiliations of men and women in contemporary America.

The implications of these conclusions we shall discuss more fully later. But first, let us ask ourselves, what do people really mean when they contend that religious instruction is necessary in order to prevent delinquency and to bolster up character? Do they not imply that good conduct is somehow foreign to human nature? That morality and character require outside support? That men are naturally prone to do the things they ought not to do and to leave undone the things they ought to do, and "there is no health in us"?

This is indeed a prevalent theory of moral conduct. We inherited it from the Puritans, who derived it in turn from the early Christians. It assumes that man is by nature corrupt, born in sin, and disposed to prefer evil to good.

But is it sound? Actually impulses to action are varied in character and are directed toward ends that are good, bad, or indifferent as time and circumstances determine. The urge to drink from the glass before me may, for example, represent a genuine need socially desirable, or it may, if gratified on a life raft adrift in mid-ocean with thirsty associates, condemn me to the level of the beast. The context is all-important. Another way of stating the point is to say that moral behavior involves more than the individual. It has to do with the way in which he relates himself to others.

To a considerable extent relationships with others involve an ordering of interests. At times the interests of one individual collide with those of his fellows, and restraint or redirection ensue. But life also affords numerous occasions for the merging of interests. Growing up in a family, or a community, means just this: the building of a self that incorporates within itself concerns shared with members of the household and the neighborhood. By identifying ourselves with interests that are initially more inclusive than ourselves, we become *members* of a family, a community, a nation. Moral growth of this character is a process of self-realization as truly as it is one of self-negation.

Character education thus requires the identification of life with life, a participation in common ways of living, working, and playing with others, a striving toward shared goals in accordance with agreed-upon standards. And while instruction—provided it has an obvious bearing on the interests involved—may exercise an important role in clarifying and interpreting and, on occasion, reconstructing ideals and principles and procedures, it is of little avail unless it is close to living experience. Again, faith without works is fruitless.

Now, all this implies in the twentieth century, here in the United States, a community of experience that both cuts through and transcends sectarian differences. The sources of our moral life are more basic than our religious affiliations. As John Stuart Mill remarked long ago, it is not religion that sustains morality; it is rather the moral life that prompts human beings to create, each for himself, or each group for itself, a religious justification for morality.

The popular notion that morality requires an underpinning in religious instruction of a sectarian character puts the cart before the horse. And, in view of the complication which is of necessity associated with the teaching of diverse religious beliefs in a school attended by the children of all the people, it is wiser for the school to concentrate upon assuring the conditions that make for adherence to the essential virtues and the moral principles that underlie the democratic way of life than to introduce religious instruction. This process requires a conscious formulation by schools of the principles they would have their pupils live by and constant provision of opportunities for young people to develop qualities of character, through practice, in harmony with those principles.

Professor John Childs has stated:

"American democracy is not only a form of government, it is also a personal and a social way of life. As a mode of individual and group life, democracy has its positive moral meanings. The social-democratic conception affirms that each and every person is worthy of respect and is never to be treated as a mere means for the advancement of the interests of others. It holds that respect for the concrete human individual necessarily involves respect for his capacities, interests, preferences, and ideas. This also involves recognition of his right, in co-operation with his fellows, to shape and reshape the institutions of his community. Moreover, according to the principles of social democracy, institutions are means; individuals are ends. The ultimate test of any institution is what it contributes to the enrichment of the lives of individual men, women, and children. This power to pass judgment on the work of the institutions under which they live is both a moral and a legal right of the citizens of a democratic society." [6]

Who will contend that these moral principles are the monopoly of any one religious sect, or that traits of character, commonly prized, traits that operate as a social cement in human relationships, are the exclusive property of one religious faith? Do they not permeate all faiths? Why then must children be divided into sectarian groups within the school or under school auspices in order to insure their acquisition? Do the honesty and reliability of John Smith, for example, derive from his Catholicism, while similar traits in Roger Jones flow from his allegiance to Methodism? Since identical traits are present in men of different religious affiliations but who share nevertheless in a basic common culture, must we not conclude that these traits are rooted more in the culture than in the peculiar philosophy of religion with which each strives to justify their exercise? [7]

Now, it is this common culture or way of life—its ideals

[6] Chapter entitled "Spiritual Values of the Secular Public School," in *The Public School and Spiritual Values,* by John S. Brubacher and others. Seventh Yearbook of the John Dewey Society. New York and London: Harper & Brothers, 1944, p. 75.

[7] In a pamphlet entitled "Spiritual Problems of the Teacher," issued by the Hazen Foundation, Ordway Tead develops a somewhat similar point of view to that above. For example, he writes suggestively:

"Despite . . . divergencies of outlook, however, one is able to discover among those who hold them wide areas of common action and of united effort. The struggle of the human community to order its affairs harmoniously in the realms of political, social, economic, medical, educational and other fields is a fact. And the effort cuts across religious bounds. What are known as 'interfaith' efforts increasingly acknowledge the need for even wider focus and collaboration. The community we tacitly seek loyalty to is *universal*. We try to make it beloved. We desire a qualitative good life to be generally shared in generous fellowship. Even and principles, its standards and practices—with which the public school is properly concerned. If some prefer to describe ideals—such as an abiding faith in the worth of each person; an equal regard for human personality irrespective of the accidents of birth; the ideal that people realize their best selves in co-operative relations with others; or the common virtues of honesty, responsibility, thoughtful and sensitive relations with one's fellows—as *religious* values, then of course religion is a requisite in the curriculum of all schools, public as well as private. But religion so conceived is altogether different from sectarian instruction.

IV

This takes us to the argument of religious liberals who, it will be recalled, insist that the schools can in-

---

the so-called 'ecumenical' devotion looks upon other religions and no religion, not to scoff nor to persecute but to understand and live with.

"Thus while the essentially theological issues are joined, the communal concerns are shared. While one man's metaphysics may be another man's verbiage, the common will to public peace, order, plenty and justice extends apace. The secularity of our day may reflect this confused metaphysics as well as deprive us of certain spiritual consolations. But that secularity has also to do with an ethical passion the height, depth and ardor of which were probably never more genuine, more inclusive nor more informed than they are today. It would be less than fair to our necessarily imperfect knowledge of ourselves not to understand that increasingly for many of us there is literally one world—not only in the international sense but in the sense of a striving for a global rule of righteousness and love. Pervading our secularity and transcending it, stands the fact of humane regard and humane endeavor. What sanctions this gets from us or we from it, what solace it brings to the lonely human heart,—these may still be problem issues of our struggling spirits. But we are, strangely or naturally and wholesomely, more united than ever in what we want to *do*. Why we have to do it and what support we get in the process—is it not here that our unities fall apart?

"I hazard, in short, that the spiritual tensions and confusions of our day arise out of uncertainties about ultimate sanctions more than out of programs. Here is a problem of who cheers us on, not as to whether we shall 'play up, play up and play the game.' "

clude religion in their programs and at the same time
exclude sectarianism. This group distinguishes between
religion as a universal function, a "valuation process" in
which all men engage, and religion as a structure with
sectarian accretions. It is religion as a function that they
wish schools to promote.

All this is very well, provided the values thus fostered
are in reality common values and not of a sectarian variety
parading in disguise. But, as we saw in the last chapter,
religion as these individuals define it and religion as
they apply it in the school are by no means identical.

Take, for example, the six ways in which they would
include religion in education.[8] Briefly summarized these
insure:

1. The acquisition of knowledge about the institutions
   of organized religion.

2. On the higher levels of education the study of religion
   as "a field of knowledge" and on the lower levels as
   an object of study in which young people come to know
   the religious roots of their culture.

3. The use of festivals in connection with seasonal events
   —Christmas, Thanksgiving, New Year's, etc.—with
   a view to the fostering of understanding and appreciation of the great religious faiths—Protestant, Catholic,
   Jewish.

4. Actual experience in the life of the school and the
   community, with a view to promoting spiritual values
   such as the worth of personality, social sensitivity, appreciation of the universe, a sense of responsibility
   and accountability, co-operative fellowship, etc.

[8] See Chapter V, pp. 95–98.

5. Exploring "the possibilities of religion as a principle of the integration of education and the culture."

6. Finally, the use of religion in personal counselling.

Clearly these suggestions are not of the same order. What secular school today fails to engage to some degree at least in the practices recommended in paragraphs one, two, and three? To know about the role of religion in history, to penetrate with imagination and appreciation into the backgrounds of our common culture, to understand in accordance with age-level and maturity the principles we cherish—and, incidentally, to observe that their validity today is not of necessity dependent upon their original justification—and to enter sympathetically into the distinctive values our associates prize, are certainly essential conditions of being educated. True, the work of the schools can improve in this area. Recent years have impressed education increasingly not only with the importance of introducing young people more consciously to the values implicit in a democratic culture but as well with the needs for intercultural education. Consequently the schools can accomplish far more than they have accomplished along these lines; but to call this orientation into values *religious* education, is to confuse matters rather than to light up the path ahead.

Similarly with suggestion four. Some pages back, mention was made of the values which emerge out of our common life, irrespective of religious and racial differences. As Brubacher and others have shown in *The Public Schools and Spiritual Values:*

"There is a large measure of agreement in American communities on what these spiritual values mean by way of actual personal conduct. Our differences, our lack of community, on them concerns rather the philosophical rationalization and verbalizing of these values." [9]

It is indeed a primary function of the school to communicate values such as respect for personality, tolerance, fraternity, love of the truth and *the disinterested search for it,* the conviction that knowledge and the power which knowledge gives should be used to promote the welfare and happiness of all, and other values we might list. It is also highly important to realize how these values are best communicated. As the writers just quoted stress:

"One learns to communicate with others—that is, one becomes a member of a community—by participating in its activities. Indeed, it is only through participation that one can be sure that he is communicating, that is, getting the same meanings out of the same symbols." [10]

But again, why need we confuse the issue by calling education of this character religious education? All values mentioned can find acceptance—and, in fact, generally do find acceptance—in an atmosphere of religious and philosophical neutrality. To be sure, on the higher levels of education, in college and graduate school, it is quite in order for the student to orient himself in religion and philosophy. This book, however, deals primarily with the elementary and secondary school, the period

[9] New York: Harper & Brothers, 1944, p. 12.
[10] *Ibid.,* p. 27.

of common education. Were the teacher of children and of young people in early adolescence to insist that the values we wish all to share acquire their validity from a supernatural order, or that they are rooted solely and exclusively in man and his environment, as the naturalists believe, he would both befuddle his pupils unnecessarily and violate injunctions against sectarian instruction.

The same reasoning holds true in regard to personal counseling—the sixth item on our list. No conscientious guidance worker can view with indifference the efforts of boys and girls to formulate a philosophy of life. But the moment he confuses their efforts to do so with his own preferences he proves false to his trust. Professional integrity requires him to respect the peculiarities of family background and the unique personality of each young person. Naturally he will act as a confidant for all who seek him out, but the resources he draws upon in order to help each and all will transcend any one parochial view of life. Varying his procedure with need and religious affiliation, he may deem it wise to refer individuals to priest or clergyman, rabbi or psychiatrist. In so doing, his purpose is to help each person to work out his own salvation, to attain a greater degree of independence and self-direction—but the path to this goal is not identical for all to travel. Rather it bears an organic relationship to the nature and the background and the present experience of each individual served. Here too an attitude of neutrality toward religious differences is a prime essential.

Suggestion five takes us head-on into difficulty. Here

the distinction between religion as a valuation process and religion as a structure breaks down. When Bower states [11] that one function of religion is to revalue "the practical interests and activities of the common life" and "to unite them into a total meaning and worth of life in terms of its responsible relation to God," and another, "to subject every practical interest and activity of the common life to cross-criticism and reconstruction in the light of this core of fundamental values," he forgets utterly the distinction he was careful to draw between religion as function and religion as structure. Politicians, as part of their stock in trade, may be privileged to use the term God as though its meanings were universally clear and identical for all. But once a teacher in a classroom seeks to determine the right and the wrong of practical activities by reference to God's injunctions, he will discover to his sorrow that neither the Deity nor his wishes are envisaged alike by all.[12]

How long, for example, would our liberals succeed in helping pupils to resolve specific problems in politics and economics, or the issues raised by science, as Bower suggests be done, "in keeping with the fatherhood of God and the brotherhood of man," without giving offense to Catholic or Jew, to Jehovah's Witness or Christian Scientist or to the members of one or more of the remaining 256 religious sects represented in our population?

And were the teacher sufficiently versatile to escape

[11] *Op. cit.,* p. 70.
[12] The reader will find it interesting to read in this connection the chapter entitled "Can the Bible Return to the Classroom?" in Conrad Moehlman's *School and Church: The American Way.*

difficulties with sects that derive their ultimate sanctions from supernatural sources—from authorities outside the natural and social order—he would still have to avoid offending the children of parents, rapidly increasing in number, who hold firmly to ideals, but conceive of the moral life as a strictly human enterprise. People of this persuasion constitute often the most intelligent members of a community. They have thought earnestly and long on the issues of life and death. From their studies they have come to the conclusion that science no longer confirms the traditional dualism of matter and mind, of body and spirit, of a natural and a supernatural order. They hold to a generous conception of human nature, a conception that runs counter to the traditional notion of man as having been born in sin, or endowed with a proneness toward evil or a natural inhibition for the good. They believe that the noble as well as the ignoble qualities in man arise out of the interrelationships of people and the forces of nature that impinge upon them. They believe, moreover, that to locate the means for ameliorating man's estate outside this vale of tears tends to undermine faith in his own resources. As one of their number, John Dewey, states:

"What is the inevitable effect of holding that anything remotely approaching a basic and serious amelioration of the human estate must be based upon means and methods that lie outside the natural and social world, while human capacities are so low that reliance upon them only makes things worse? Science cannot help; industry and commerce cannot help; political and jural arrangements cannot help; ordinary affections, sympathies and friendship cannot help. Place these natural resources under the terrible handicap put upon them by every mode of anti-naturalism, and what is the outcome? Not that these things have not accomplished anything in fact, but that their operation has always been weakened and hampered in just the degree in which supernaturalism has prevailed." [13]

My concern here is not with the truth or falsity of naturalism or supernaturalism. It is rather the fact, which advocates of religion in education commonly overlook, that naturalism as well as supernaturalism has a sizable following and is entitled to respect in our schools. In the latter part of the nineteenth century, Protestants found it necessary to organize the public school so that it would deal fairly with Catholics and Jews as well as Protestants. The same principles of justice require today the recognition of large numbers of citizens who no longer are at home within traditional religious organizations. And, if we may judge by the steadily increasing number and the present size of the unchurched population (approximately 56 per cent of our total population) the naturalists constitute both a respectable and a substantial section of our citizens. Moreover, to imply that the children of these people, merely because they are unchurched, are a menace to society or to themselves, or that their parents are unmindful and neglectful of their spiritual health, is to brand oneself as intolerant or grossly uninformed or both.

It seems then that morality, by which is meant specifically the moral principles which all of us, young and

[13] "Anti-Naturalism in Extremis," *Partisan Review*, X (January-February, 1943), p. 33.

old, live by in our day-by-day relationships in family and community, in state and nation, yes, even in the relations of nation with nation, requires no sectarian emphasis in our schools. Sectarian instruction in religion is not needed in order that our children may sense the values, and mold their lives in the image, of sound morality. Nor is religious instruction indispensable in order to promote the democratic way of life. This, as we have seen, we inherit from many sources, and, if it is to remain vital, it will create new forms and qualities of human relationships in the future.

Both morality and democracy are, however, rooted in our common culture. They are the inheritance and the promise of all, without respect to differences in nationality, economic circumstance, race, color, or creed. Consequently, sectarian instruction in religion is not necessary in order to improve the moral fiber of our children or to ground them in a healthy allegiance to democracy. Moreover, there are positive dangers in the tendency to introduce religion into public education, as there are dangers in yielding to the demands, growing in volume, that the state use its resources in order to assist non-public schools. These dangers constitute the subject matter of the next two chapters.

Chapter VII

HOW RELIGIOUS TEACHING
COMPROMISES THE TASK OF THE SCHOOL

SEVERAL conclusions emerge from the last chapter. First, it is not essential to import religious teachings into the school in order to bring up young people to be of sound character or to imbue them with democratic principles. Second, the common virtues and the moral principles implicit in democracy are the offspring of a cultural environment that is both more inclusive and more potent than any one parochial conception of life. It is from this sustaining culture that morality derives its vigor. Finally, it was suggested not only that the schools can develop moral character independently of sectarian instruction, but that it is highly important for them to do so.

I now wish to draw attention to serious complications associated with the attempt of religious organizations to gain admission to the public school.

II

First to suffer are the children in whose behalf instruction presumably is given. The moment children are separated the one from the other along religious lines, they are made conscious of differences which have no place in the public school. Try as the school may, the child of a religious minority or of the unchurched will cringe before the finger of deviation that so cruelly points him out. The remarks of Reverend Philip Schug of Urbana, Illinois, in this connection are enlightening. Reverend Schug was so moved by the effects of religious segregation upon the children that he advised one parent, a Mrs. V. McCollum, to challenge the legality of sectarian teaching in tax-supported schools during school hours. Says he:

"I, being a minister who has taken an active interest in religious education and who helped build a successful department of religious education in my own church where none has existed for many years, can understand the zeal and missionary fervor with which this invasion of the schools began. I can sympathize with the frustrations experienced by religious people who have seen their world split asunder. But I do not agree that the solution—taking over public school classes, dividing the children into two, three, four or more different groups, and instructing them separately in varying religious philosophies is a wise solution. Many problems arise. To illustrate, the problem of the direct teaching from divisions into different groups is a most serious one. Religious instruction is the only instruction for which children must be so divided. The public school is a great agent for democracy in that rich and poor, Jew and Gentile, and all social classes unite for common activity. It breaks down divisions, but when sectarian religious instruction is added it automatically teaches division and becomes an active agent in creating frictions.

"Indeed, it was just this which brought Mrs. McCollum

to me. Her boy, Terry, was ostracized and ridiculed by his classmates because he did not take religious instruction. For a child there is probably no punishment more severe or more serious than being shunned and ridiculed by his fellows. Yet it is inevitable that such things will happen when sectarian teachers take a natural school group and divide the sheep from the goats and then subdivide the sheep for instruction in conflicting philosophies. Such a program of education, in my estimation, is basically unsound and destructive of the finer values regardless of the high hopes and good intentions of the instructors." [1]

Nor does the persecution of the minority child end with the classroom experience. Separation of the sheep from the goats in one area extends naturally to other areas, and thus docs religious differentiation lead to incidents on the playground and the street which contravene our democratic tenets. Nor is any sect or any racial group wholly safe when we take into consideration the country as a whole, since the majority in one locality is commonly a minority in another; and scarcely a community exists without a minority child in its midst. At some time or in some place the children of each religious sect are subject to the corroding influences of a sense of difference.

Nor are all teachers sufficiently wise to be trusted with the responsibility of directing pupils to classes on religion. From all parts of the country, where classes are permitted in the school building or pupils are dismissed on school time for instruction in church schools, come reports of abuses of the rights of children as well as the

---

[1] Statement from "The Case of Mrs. V. McCollum *vs.* The Champaign, Illinois, School Board," issued by the Chicago Action Council, 1945.

rights of parents to enjoy religious freedom without discrimination. On occasion teachers exercise questionable pressure openly; as, for example, in Buffalo, New York. David Diamond, a lawyer in that city, writes:

"I was corporation counsel of the city of Buffalo when the question of released time arose. I was opposed to granting it on all the grounds which your investigation discloses but I was asked only for a legal opinion. Of course, at the time, my objections were based on opinion. I know now they were statements of fact. Many examples of the damage resulting locally could be cited. One will suffice.

"Some of the more stupid teachers lined up against different walls of their classrooms the children of the various faiths, in order to classify them. And so these little ones stared across the room at each other—the Catholics at the Protestants, the latter at the former and both at the Jews. These children, for the first time in their short lives, were made conscious of alleged differences among themselves. The results have been the expected ones.

"The administrative problems which have arisen are legion, the irritations numerous." [2]

Incidents of this character are by no means peculiar to Buffalo. In New York City, for example, the Public Education Association has conducted several surveys of the administration of the released-time program. These reveal repeated violations of neutrality on the part of teachers, instances in which teachers virtually require children to enroll in religious classes, even though the regulations of the Board of Education specifically forbid so doing.

[2] In "Personal and Otherwise," *Harper's Magazine,* June, 1944.

At times the pressure exerted by the school is more subtle, and children and parents alike realize that discretion is the better part of valor and, in order to avoid unpleasant experiences, decide to conform.

Church groups commonly expect, naïvely in some instances, less so in others, that the public schools will assist them in the initial task of enrolling children in religious classes and in following up enrollment with the enforcement of attendance. This necessarily involves both time and expense. In a large city school system it requires a considerable drain upon personnel, even though to use public employees for this purpose is in violation of the law, which commonly forbids both the appropriation and the use of school funds on behalf of the interests of religious sects. The Citizens' School Committee of Chicago, Illinois, quite properly objects to this practice in the following words:

"As soon as any church is allowed to conduct classes in a school building or school funds are expended to keep records, check truancy, or exercise control over the quality of instruction in such classes, there is a clear violation of our state constitution. Even to excuse children from school, except between the ages of 12 and 14 for confirmation classes, violates the school attendance law of Illinois." [3]

I might remark parenthetically that an ironical situation exists in Illinois. On the one hand, earnest citizens insist that religious instruction is needed in order to safeguard and promote moral character and obedience to law. On the other, these selfsame citizens encourage

[3] *Chicago's Schools,* XII, No. 1 (August, 1945). Published by Citizens' School Committee.

the dismissal of children from school for purposes of religious education, in clear violation of the law of the state.

Not only are the children of parents who refuse to co-operate in religious instruction subject to discrimination and to character-degrading experiences. They are commonly prevented from using the released-time period constructively. As the Citizens' Committee in Chicago points out, "It is the avowed expectation of those who favor the plan that children who remain in school must not be taught anything essential, and in many schools it is actually the classwork of the majority that must be curtailed." [4]

What to do with the children who elect not to attend religious classes constitutes an embarrassing problem for school people. Should they decide to use the released-time period for interesting and valuable work, such as special periods in the arts and crafts, or dramatic play, or special assistance in academic work, they are accused of competing unfairly with the religious classes and detracting from enrollments in the latter. Or should they attempt, as some schools have done, to provide instruction in ethics during this hour, their efforts are interpreted as unfriendly and designed to undermine religious instruction.

All this renders it hard for a school administrator. Exposed as he is to the pressure of religious groups eager to enlarge their church membership lists or to use the school in order to identify through their lambs the wayward ewes of the community—who may thus be made

[4] *Ibid.*

to return to the fold—he finds it difficult indeed to steer a neutral course. Particularly is this true in communities where religious sects are unevenly distributed. In one community, for example, the children each fall receive from the school an enrollment blank which they must present to their parents. This blank contains instructions for their parents to check one of two statements: (1) "I wish my child to receive religious instruction"; (2) "I do not wish my child to receive religious instruction." Actually, however, only two well-established religious denominations exist in the community. Consequently, the choice confronting the parents boils down to religious instruction at the hands of either Catholics or Lutherans, or none at all. Obviously a decision to refuse religious instruction to the child identifies him as being nonconformist. Is it surprising that the children of dissenting parents are subjected to taunts and jeers on the playground and the street, or that other parents permit their children to enroll in the classes of a religious faith which they themselves cannot accept?

Organizing classes in religion on school time necessarily reduces further the time available in schools to meet the demands of a curriculum already badly crowded. Religious groups are not the only ones to see in the school a convenient opportunity to reach all the children of all the people. Other agencies—more legitimately—turn to the school in order to convey information or to develop habits and attitudes essential for both individual and community well-being. Safety education, education for international-mindedness, work experience, co-operation in all-community projects, are illustrations of what is meant. Adding provision for religious education complicates a badly tangled schedule. Frequently the time for releasing children varies with the different churches; or, when religious instructors operate within the school, classes are necessarily interspersed throughout the day, since the personnel available does not permit all to meet simultaneously. Try as a conscientious administrator will, awkward interruptions of work ensue, to the impairment of the normal work of the school.

The legitimate objections to the released-time program are well summarized in the conclusions of a survey conducted in California in October 1945. This was the second of two surveys made by the Public Education Society of San Francisco and covered the operations of the program in fifty-seven of the cities of California. The Association's conclusions are as follows:

"The plan is a failure in California's Public Schools measured by any conceivable yardstick.

"In a democracy no plan or law should be adopted which does not have the approval of a MAJORITY of our people. The fairest evidence after ample trial is that only about a third of the eligible elementary school pupils use the plan, and less than an eighth of the eligible high school students use the plan.

"It is unwise to disrupt the school instruction of a majority of a class for the special wishes of a minority on a religious issue. Article 1 of the Bill of Rights guarantees the separation of Church and State. Many superintendents share the view that the Released Time Plan is a flagrant violation of the spirit if not the letter of the Constitution of the United States and the laws of the State of California.

"Most unfortunate is the fact that the plan discriminates against those of Jewish faith and many Protestant denominations, because no nearby church of their denomination is within walking distance of the school.

"In most cases neither the teacher nor the public has been consulted before the Released Time Plan has been put into operation. The public pays for and maintains the public schools and sends their children there by reason of political or religious convictions. The teachers are held responsible to the public for good education, still the vital matter of encroachment of the Church upon the schools has been taken completely and arbitrarily out of their hands.

"A child is in public school only one-ninth of the year and there is eight-ninths of the year, including summer vacations, in which to give week-day religious education. There is little or no excuse for disrupting the public school program for Released Time Plans which tend to make the public schools a police arm of the Churches.

"Because it works a severe injustice to those adherents of several religions the plan is discriminatory, shortsighted, unjust and un-American and doomed to inevitable failure. The figures point to a trend that the plan will fail.

"The Public Education Society of San Francisco again points out that the plan has failed here as it has in the nation as a whole and again urges its abandonment where in use and its complete exclusion from San Francisco's schools.

"The survey of October 1945 shows that in California, as in nearly forty other states, a well-meaning legislature has yielded to religious pressure groups, no doubt because it lacked complete acquaintance with the facts."

Finally, religious instruction is in danger of encouraging school authorities to delegate a responsibility for the moral education of children that is uniquely their own. If school people as well as men and women outside the schools accept the fallacious notion that moral education requires the support of sectarian teaching, schools will be tempted to delegate to others the task which they alone are admirably equipped to perform: the task of cultivating ideals, standards, and ways of living in young people who vary in religion, in race, in nationality, and in socio-economic status.

Of this I shall have more to say in the last chapter. Let us now observe how religious teaching compromises the school in its attempt to discipline the mind.

III

Since Colonial days this country has comprised a heterogeneous population. True, people who sought refuge in America or who felt impelled to push ever westward in order to breathe a more congenial atmosphere have tended to establish themselves in homogeneous communities. But these communities have failed to remain long of one racial, religious, or political complexion. The Mormons could no more keep to themselves in the deserts of Utah than could the residents of the Oneida community on the attractive soil of western New York. The steady improvement of means of transportation and of communication have rendered futile attempts at isolation and insulated ways of living.

Moreover, in time assimilation became a positive ideal. Following the Revolutionary War, Americans became more concerned with developing the potentialities of life on this continent than with the maintenance of cultural connections abroad. The conditions of survival and of success alike, on the frontier, favored the evolution of common ideals and common patterns of behavior; and it soon came to matter little to the second and third generation of the foreign born where one's parents originated.

Meager as were the facilities of public education throughout the greater portion of the nineteenth century, the school served likewise as a potent factor in assimilation. A major purpose yesterday, as today, was to bridge the gap that separates individuals of diverse backgrounds—to create unity while fostering a respect for differences, and, on occasion, to stimulate the differences that add to the spice of life.

The ideal of assimilation was furthered also by the dominance of young people in our population. Young people are not afraid of change. Indeed they welcome change and are eager to possess themselves of the tools with which to reconstruct their environment. Particularly has this been true in this country, where change and an education that equips for change have meant an opportunity to alter one's status in life. All through our history the school has been a conscious instrument for raising children above the station in life in which they were born.

Finally the two necessities, assimilation and an educational program that faces the future hopefully, received reinforcement from the American political tradition with its philosophy of natural rights, particularly the rights of freedom of thought and expression, as embodied in the Federal and state constitutions and ordinances governing new territories.

These three aspects of education reinforce the importance of equipping young people with tools of inquiry and disciplined methods of thinking which they can use in flexible ways to resolve their difficulties and to evolve new and creative solutions of old problems. They emphasize the importance of tools with which to work, in preference to specific answers to specific questions. And so it has come about that Americans envisage their schools less as places in which to amass knowledge as such and more as sources where they can acquire the basic principles, the attitudes and the skills with which to steer one's course in an uncertain world—a world of hazard and promise alike. And whenever education in elementary or secondary school or college has seemed to bog down with routine, or to indoctrinate, or to value subject matter more highly than the development of the power that makes for flexible adjustments to life, it has come under severe indictment. Likewise when pressure groups outside the school seek to use education for their own selfish ends, to influence instruction so as to create preordained conclusions, the friends of education ground their defense of the integrity of teaching in the traditional ideal of education for the open mind.

Now, the effort to bring religion into the schools runs directly counter to this well-established tradition.

I referred a moment ago to the philosophy of natural rights which, since the Declaration of Independence, has been central in the American political tradition. The natural rights of men, in the minds of Thomas Jefferson and other leading thinkers of the eighteenth century, derived directly from nature and nature's God. To quote Carl L. Becker:

"The mysterious ways in which God moved to perform his wonders, so far from being known through official and dogmatic pronouncements of church and state, were to be progressively discovered by the free play of human reason upon accumulated and verifiable knowledge. The free play of human reason, given time enough, could therefore discover the invariable laws of nature and nature's God and, by bringing the ideas and the institutions of man into conformity with them, find the way, as Volney said, to perfection and happiness." [5]

Accordingly, faith in the ability of untrammeled thinking to arrive at truth and thus to insure happiness was a powerful antidote against the dogmatic and sectarian rivalry which threatened often to perpetuate discord and conflict in American life. And while, as Becker also shows, Americans no longer accept in their original form the assumptions that underlay the doctrine of natural rights, they "are still betting that freedom of the mind will never disprove the proposition that only through freedom of the mind can a reasonably just society ever be created." [6]

It is true that the doctrine of natural rights no longer rests comfortably on its early philosophical and religious foundations. Moreover, both the theory and the practice of free speech and free inquiry encounter difficulties today that did not occur to Jefferson and his colleagues.

[5] *Freedom and Responsibility in the American Way of Life.* New York: Alfred A. Knopf, 1945, p. 31.
[6] *Ibid.*, p. 42.

However, as the original foundations for the doctrine began to crumble, new support was found for the principle of reason and rational methods of inquiry. This new ally was modern science. By its works science with its controlled and refined methods of thinking—particularly its objective and disinterested procedure in searching for and testing truth—has established itself as an indispensable tool, if not an inherent aspect, of democracy.

Not only an indispensable tool but one that alone makes for responsibility in decisions! One of the hazards of free expression in modern society is the ease with which it is abused. Few people can take the time to investigate the accuracy of the news they read in newspaper or magazine; and the instruments of propaganda, aided by increasingly effective means of communication, render it easy for the propagandist to excite the mass mind with false information and clever manipulation of prejudice and emotion. No satisfactory device exists at present to protect the consumer of information against adulterated products. But to the degree that the average citizen is trained to detect the wiles of the propagandist, to weigh evidence and to draw conclusions only so far as the data in hand warrant, the evils of a laissez-faire economy in ideas will be offset by the self-imposed regulations of controlled thinking.

At least this is the hope of all who wish to avoid public censorship of the mind. Our fathers recognized early the dependence of free government upon education. As early as 1816 the Constitution of Indiana declared:

"Knowledge and learning generally diffused through a community being essential to the preservation of a free government . . . it shall be the duty of the general assembly . . . to provide by law for a system of education, ascending in regular gradation from township schools to a state university, wherein tuition shall be gratis, and equally open to all." [7]

Early in our history Governor Berkeley of Virginia exclaimed, "Thank God, there are no free schools or printing" (in the colony under his jurisdiction). Thus did he hope to prevent disobedience and any questioning of his rule. But in the course of the years Americans have adopted precisely the opposite policy and have written into their constitutions the natural right of men to speak and write their minds and to think their own thoughts. A logical consequence of this guarantee of the free mind for citizens is the maintenance of free schools dedicated to the task of preparing the minds and the dispositions of young people to exercise this freedom in full consciousness of the obligations it entails.

In the last chapter I shall outline in some detail the obligation of the school to develop not only the minds of young people but other aspects of their nature as well. But here I wish to call attention to the sacred trust thus imposed upon the school—a corollary of the principle of separation of church and state. This trust is to equip young people so that they can assume not only the privileges but the responsibilities of free citizens in a free society. To turn to Carl Becker once again:

[7] Quoted by Carl L. Becker, *op. cit.*, p. 44.

"In the long history of civilization there have been relatively few systems of government that accepted in theory and applied in practice the dangerous notion that learning and teaching should be perfectly free. Modern liberal democracy is one of the few. In theory at least, however much or little it may apply the theory in practice, it rests upon the right of the individual to freedom of learning and teaching." [8]

There is no right, however, without a corresponding duty. A necessary accompaniment of the *right* to think freely is to learn to exercise skill in thinking. Consequently, the intellectual responsibility of general education in our democracy is, at its minimum, to acquaint young people with the information and knowledge essential to enable the intelligent citizen to find his way around in the modern world; and to develop reasonable skill in reflective thinking, the skill that emerges out of practice in defining and formulating problems, in gathering facts on which to base inferences, hypotheses, and generalizations, in testing and verifying these "guesses," and in applying the results of inference with a tentative attitude of mind which realizes that new data and further insight into the methods of proof employed may tomorrow require a revision of conclusions.

In these days of a revival of intolerance we cannot overemphasize the crucial importance of education in the scientific attitude. And while crimes have been committed in the name of science—overly enthusiastic and outright dogmatic affirmations regarding the nature of man which offend against the spirit of science even in its name—we should not allow these mistakes to blind

8 *Ibid.,* p. 45.

us to the role that scientific procedure must play in all schools that profess to prepare their students for democratic living. The wise teacher will, of course, temper his instruction to the shorn lamb. Growth in experience and social maturity in elementary and secondary school and in college will call for different degrees and gradations in teaching; but the point to stress is that on all levels the training in thinking that leads eventually to self-direction in the use of the mind is a primary function in democratic education. Given this preparation, it literally follows that education will make men free.

Obviously, since schools in the United States are locally supported and controlled, school districts will vary in their conception of "proper" freedom of teaching and learning. An essential freedom in one community is considered undesirable license in another. Communities also vary in their interpretations of what constitute the "minimum essentials" of information, skill, and moral character. By and large they do agree fairly well, however, on the fundamental characteristics of personality, and on the moral principles implicit in our democracy, which they would have schools develop—even though these selfsame principles quite properly become the subject matter of critical evaluation in college and graduate school.

Educators have also developed a technique of teaching appropriate to situations of a controversial character. In economics or politics or problems in social relations, where truth is not as yet salted down (that is, verified beyond a reasonable doubt), the good teacher helps his students distinguish between the principles, upon which there frequently is agreement, that are embedded in controversial issues, and the rival solutions that seem to follow upon the application of these principles. Thus they can properly develop an allegiance to shared values while fostering the open mind with respect to "right answers." For example, it is not the function of the school to answer specifically the problem of employment; but it is its function to render young people sensitive alike to the facts of unemployment and to the basic principle that society is responsible for the welfare of its members. That is, the school should lay bare the basic principles and the common goals upon which men are of one mind, as distinguished from the areas of controversy that emerge once the principles are employed in the search for specific solutions of mooted questions.

The difference between basic principles and specific conclusions is illustrated in the study of government. No school can wisely omit acquainting its pupils with the tenets of the major political parties. Indeed, in some communities with a high order of intelligence, children are introduced as well to rival systems of government, such as Fascism, Communism, Democracy! The minimum of tolerance would seem to permit young people learning to distinguish, with the help of the school, between the donkey and the elephant and the convictions of a Democrat and a Republican! But were a school to delegate its responsibility in this area to the leaders of the local Democratic, Republican, or Communist Parties, most of us would infer that it had shirked a task clearly its own. And if, in addition, children were segregated for this purpose on the basis of the party affiliations of their parents, would we not conclude that the school had indeed gone bankrupt?

On what ground would we object to this procedure? Is it not because we believe partisan instruction has no place in the public school? We should not question the right of a parent of passionate convictions to instruct his child quite apart from the school in the doctrines of the Democratic Party. That is his privilege as a citizen and a parent. But the extent to which the school might go in this matter would be only to seek conviction on principles of government common to all parties and mere knowledge about the objectives and goals of rival political organizations.

Are not religion and public education in a similar relation? And when we segregate children in schools or on a released-time program that is fostered by the school for the purpose of indoctrinating them in different religious faiths, is not the school as a school equally guilty of educational malpractice? As we shall see later, there is a minimum of information and knowledge about the religious institutions and organizations of a community which the school can convey without violating the spirit of neutrality to which the school as the representative of the state is committed. One major purpose of this orientation, however, is to foster common understandings and mutual appreciation, to wear down the rough edges of religious suspicion and antagonism so often conveyed to children by their parents. In these days of group tension this purpose is highly important and is obviously achieved best without segregation. Indeed, the presence in the same classroom of representatives of different faiths affords the wise teacher an excellent opportunity to use the contributions of the children themselves in developing a positive tolerance.

The school, in matters of religion, should not go beyond this exchange of information and the furthering of attitudes of mutual respect. Instruction designed to bring commitment to one religion or another belongs outside the school.

Far wiser is it to heed the words of John Dewey written in 1908, when religious forces were just beginning to seek the return of religious education to the school:

"Bearing in mind the losses and inconveniences of our time as best we may, it is the part of men to labor persistently and patiently for the clarification and development of the positive creed of life implicit in democracy and in science, and to work for the transformation of all practical instrumentalities of education till they are in harmony with these ideas. Till these ends are further along than we can honestly claim them to be at present, it is better that our schools should do nothing than that they should do wrong things. It is better for them to confine themselves to their obvious urgent tasks than that they should, under the name of spiritual culture, form habits of mind which are at war with the habits of mind congruous with democracy and with science. It is not laziness nor cynicism which calls for this policy; it is honesty, courage, sobriety, and faith." [9]

9 "The Schools and Religion," in *John Dewey's Philosophy*, edited by Joseph Ratner. New York: Modern Library, 1939, p. 706.

Chapter VIII

SHALL THE STATE ASSIST NON-PUBLIC SCHOOLS?

A S WE saw in Chapter V, organized religion asks more of the state than to foster religious instruction in the schools. Pressure of a steadily increasing character is being brought to bear upon state legislatures and the Congress of the United States to subsidize parochial schools. These efforts have already borne fruit. In a number of states the school bus transports children free of charge to the parochial as well as the public school. Health services are extended to children in sectarian and secular school alike. Not satisfied with the assistance received in areas somewhat remote from instruction, ever more urgent voices are raised in favor of the state's supplying additional help in the form of free textbooks, subsidies for teachers' salaries, and appropriations for building and maintenance.

Nor are these labors altogether barren of results. As indicated earlier, the United States Supreme Court has validated legislation which obligates the state to furnish free textbooks to parochial schools; [1] and for some years repeated efforts have been made in the United States

[1] The court ruled, however, that the textbooks supplied children are to be identical with those used in public schools and are not to contain sectarian doctrines.

Congress to include appropriations to "non-public" as well as public schools in connection with proposals to equalize education in the states through Federal aid. A typical attempt of this character was the Mead-Aiken Bill (S. 717) which was introduced in the Seventy-ninth Congress. This bill would authorize the distribution of Federal funds to non-public schools for the construction of buildings, transportation, library facilities, textbooks "and other reading materials," "visual aids and other instructional materials, school health programs and facilities, and other necessary projects." [2]

Since the movement to provide public aid for religious schools gains momentum rapidly, it is of first importance to review the arguments advanced in its behalf. What leads people to favor doing today precisely the opposite of what President Grant, in his message to Congress on December 7, 1875, urged should be prohibited to state and Federal government alike by Constitutional amendment?

First is the practical consideration that parochial schools are losing ground in competition with public schools. As Conrad H. Moehlman has shown,[3] both Catholic and Protestant parochial schools are failing to hold the children of their respective religious persuasions. Referring to the religious census of 1936, he states: "A Protestant constituency of over thirty-one million can muster only a paltry 275,643 enrollment for all its paro-

[2] It is interesting to observe that in order to grant assistance to sectarian schools the term "non-public" is used. The Mead-Aiken bill would have benefited the most exclusive and expensive private schools, were they shrewd enough to incorporate as nonprofit corporations, as well as sectarian schools operating below the subsistence level.

[3] *Church and State, The American Way,* chapters v and vi.

chial schools, while over twenty-six million pupils attend
public schools. The Protestant parochial school has col-
lapsed." [4] With respect to Catholics, he points out that
in 1936 there were only slightly more than 2,000,000 children between the ages of five and seventeen in parochial
schools, out of at least 4,650,061 Catholic children under thirteen years of age. In other words, it is fair to say
"that more than two million Roman Catholic children
under thirteen years of age are not attending parochial
schools." [5] Since the Jews are well served in religious
education by the supplementary afternoon weekday
school, the Sunday religious school, and the all-day
parochial school, they are seemingly content to let the
public school remain a secular institution.[6] Consequently
we encounter from Jewish quarters little or no demand
for either a program of released time or state subsidies for
church schools.[7] Pressure of this character emanates
chiefly from Catholic and Protestant sources.

The latter are impelled in large measure by fear, and
they admit frankly that without financial help from the
state their schools will continue to diminish in importance and their membership to shrink in size. Such
an outcome, they contend, militates against public welfare. Consequently they ask Americans to re-examine
traditional conceptions of the relation of school and state.

[4] *Ibid.*, p. 68.

[5] *Ibid.*, p. 79.

[6] According to Israel S. Chipkin, about 70 per cent of Jewish children
receive instruction during their school age. Cf. *Twenty-five Years of Jewish Education in the United States,* Jewish Education Association of
New York City, New York, 1937; also J. Paul Williams, *op. cit.,* pp. 76–80.

[7] Cf. "Released Time for Religious Study," by Morris Fine in *Contemporary Jewish Record,* IV (February, 1941), p. 20.

J. Paul Williams, for example, argues that the extension of public assistance to denominational schools in no way impairs religious freedom. As evidence he cites European practice where the state lends financial aid to denominational institutions. Moreover, since in these schools, as well as in government schools where religious instruction is given, parents who object to religious instruction are not required to subject their children to it, Williams contends that full religious freedom is assured. And, inasmuch as government assistance is meted out to any and all denominations with membership lists large enough to warrant establishing a school—the government often assuming the full cost of denominational schools—he believes the principle of separation of church and state is in no way contravened.[8]

This argument overlooks two very important considerations. In the first place, education in Europe has scarcely emancipated itself as yet from the control of religion. Indeed, the separation of church and state, as we know it in the United States, hardly exists in Europe —with the possible exception of France.[9] Consequently, an appeal to European precedent is like insisting that we return to conditions obtaining in America prior to the Civil War.

Second, public education as a public function has not attained a status in Europe similar to that in the United States. The public school, as a school for the

8 Williams, *op. cit.*, chapter IV.

9 Nor is the situation in France altogether analogous to that in the United States, because of the difference between the circumstances under which France resolved to free its public schools from association with the Catholic Church, and those under which the nonsectarian and later the secular schools evolved in the United States.

children of all the people, is still in its infancy. In the United States, on the other hand, the vast majority of the population of school age attends the public school, and a relatively small minority non-public schools of all descriptions. Consequently, to hold up European practice as a model for adoption in the United States is to ask our people to retrace the long and at times painful journey they have traveled, not only in bringing about the separation of church and state, but in developing a genuine and a unique system of public education.

Nor is it adequate from an educational point of view to argue that religious freedom is conserved in schools that provide religious instruction, as long as the children of dissenters can exempt themselves from classes on religion. This argument misses the point entirely. The question is not whether the *parent* shall be free to excuse his child from classes in religion. It is rather the right of a child to an education in an atmosphere free from discrimination and segregation and the searing effects upon his personality of a sense of difference from his fellows. Once a child crosses the threshold of the public school, this school owes to him the full support of all its resources in becoming one with other children, Americans all, without the handicap of accentuated differences in race, color, creed, or nationality. To emphasize rather than to reconcile these distinctions in the school is to offend against the moral and the educational principles implicit in a democratic education.

There is still a third difference between education in this country and abroad which Americans must not forget. Education in Europe, by and large, grows out of an assumed or actual homogeneity in population. In each country there is a dominant culture and a settled tradition, if not an established religion, that clearly identifies the majority of the people. This predominant culture with its accepted religion tends to pervade public education. Consequently, religious freedom consists in the right to deviate therefrom. In the United States, in theory, and to a considerable extent in practice, our culture is still in the making. The facts of heterogeneity rather than homogeneity have given character to our practices. Even in Colonial days, when church and state were united, the colonies differed one from the other in the denomination of the state's choice. In New England the Congregational Church walked hand in hand with the state government; in Virginia the Episcopal Church was favored. To this early disparity as between the colonies have been added the effects of immigration, so that in virtually every state the religious affiliations of our people resemble a coat of many colors. For a time these conflicting loyalties in religion constituted a grave danger to unity. On the whole, however, Americans are a hospitable people and are prone to accept one another. Consequently, the rough edges of religious and racial difference tend to wear down. The custom of excluding religious instruction from the school, together with a corresponding emphasis upon a community of ideals that both transcend and permeate differences in religion, nationality, and race, has enabled public education to accomplish miracles in the way of welding one people out of otherwise dissident elements. To reverse this

trend at precisely the moment when there is an ominous
resurgence of intolerance and antagonism in our population is as hazardous as the attempt to put out a fire by
casting oil upon it.

II

Individuals who suggest the adoption of European
practice with respect to religious education pave the
way for the more extreme position of Catholic educators. Catholics have long contended that education is
a church and a family concern; that it is the function of
the state to support education rather than itself to conduct education. A recent article by John E. Wise, S.J.,
of Loyola College, Baltimore, forcefully restates the
Catholic argument. Wise, like Williams, draws attention
to practice abroad. For example, he writes:

"Democracy is for all the people. England, Canada, Hol-
land, Scotland have solved the problem better than we. There
the irreligious do not win out. They may have their own
schools, but are not allowed to prescribe schools for other
people's children. The case of Scotland is in point. . . .

"The arrangements proposed placed teachers under the
state for qualifications and certification, and under the
Church for approval concerning religious belief and character. Obviously there was great trust on all sides, and good
will. But now, since 1918, the general situation in Scotland is
that every Catholic child is taught by Catholic teachers in a
Catholic school. The right of parents to choose the school for
their children is guarded and protected, and does not become
inoperative, as it can in the United States when the parents
or the parishes lack money. Presbyterians, the most numer-

ous group in Scotland, have their schools, and the Episco-palians theirs." [10]

Wise evidently believes that the best defense is an offense. Consequently, in holding to the position that the state should take over the financing of the education of Catholic children in Catholic schools, he indicts the secular school as irreligious. The earnest endeavor of American educators, most of whom were men of profound religious conviction, to develop a school which would introduce young people to their common culture and carefully avoid indoctrination in areas where universal conviction does not exist, now becomes "the dictation of the antireligious"! He exclaims:

"The advocates of secularism win out. . . . God has no real place in the state school. However one may wish to qual-ify this remark, it seems incontestable, if God is important at all. The doctrine of religious indifferentism is represented in the state school, but the doctrines of Judaism, Protestant-ism, Mohammedism, and Catholicism are not. This is not democracy." [11]

Were this charge of godlessness not so commonly leveled by many Catholics against the secular public school, I should not mention it here. It is one of the most deplorable and inexcusable methods to employ for the purpose of destroying confidence in public education. Would that all departments of the state were staffed by men and women of an integrity, an earnestness, and high ideals equal, by and large, to those of the teachers of our public schools!

[10] "Federal Aid for Religious Schools," *School and Society*, LXII (Dec. 8, 1945), p. 364.
[11] *Ibid.*, p. 364.

Nor are the schools indifferent to moral values. One country-wide characteristic of recent revisions in courses of study and in curriculum organization is the emphasis given to the development of sensitive and healthy personalities through the resources of the school. Both subject matter and methods of working in the classroom are envisaged increasingly as means with which to foster character. This is a proper function of public education; and to the extent that education can accomplish this end —certainly in the elementary and in the early years of the secondary school—without reference to rival religious philosophies and conflicting creeds, the better will it serve the common welfare. To contend that the omission of explicit indoctrination in religion is the equivalent of "denying God" is to exemplify a logic strange and wonderful to behold!

But to return to Wise's argument. His program is simple. Let the state rebate to Catholics and, by inference, to other religious groups, their proportionate shares of tax receipts now used to maintain public schools.

"Catholic taxes for Catholic children in Catholic schools might well be a motto for one group, however much other religious groups subscribe or do not subscribe to the need for religious schools. The Supreme Law of the land recognizes the right of the parent to choose the school for the child. Just as clear and just as undeniable is the right to a proportionate share of taxes." [12]

Obviously, if we accept the principle that taxpayers may organize in groups and withdraw from the public treasury amounts in proportion to sums paid in, we must

[12] *Ibid.*, p. 364.

condone the tendency to neglect the underprivileged population in our cities not only in education but in health facilities, police protection, and other essential services of a public character. Do we in fact justify this discrimination? Do we not hold rather that a just and a democratic state requires its citizens to pay taxes in accordance with their ability to pay and provides services in proportion to need? And would Catholics, in point of fact, adhere consistently to this principle, once it were in effect? Suppose, for example, the Catholic population in a given community were large in numbers but poor in worldly goods. Would it be proper to confine expenditures for the education of Catholic children to the amounts derived from the Catholic population? Clearly not. Then something is wrong with the principles suggested.

The fact is, education is not the exclusive concern of parents or of the church to which parents belong. In the United States education is a state function, and the obligations of education as a state function transcend the religious interest, important and even sacred as this concern may otherwise be. It is the obligation of the state to provide for all children the type of education that will insure to them a healthy physical, intellectual, social, and emotional development as well as an effective participation in our common culture. Moreover, so important is education to a free society that the state taxes all its citizens in behalf of education without respect to whether or not they be married or single, are blessed with children or are childless. So important also is education to the well-being of the state, that we have built up in

this country a public school system which, despite its
failures, is unmatched by that of any other country on
the globe. In no country where public funds for education are distributed—I am tempted to say dissipated!—
amongst religious groups, is public education so effi-
ciently or so effectively conducted as in the United States.

What in fact is being proposed is the destruction of
our public schools without corresponding gains. It is
sought to withdraw the funds which they now use without discrimination in the interests of children and to
divert these sums to the support of sectarian institutions.
Imagine, for example, the effects upon the public school
systems in the United States if any considerable number
of the 256 religious sects were privileged to develop
schools at public expense. Public schools would wither
and die without any assurance whatsoever of adequate
replacement. Indeed, the dissipation of energy and talent
and resources consequent upon the multiplication of
sectarian schools would in itself militate against effectiveness. The overlapping and duplication of facilities required would multiply the cost of education per capita,
service for service, with no guarantee of improvement in
the quality of education.

Here again there is an obvious difference between
educational conditions in Europe and the United States.
The effort in Europe to broaden the base of popular
education and to move in the direction of general and
universal education in elementary and secondary schools
may benefit for a time from a policy of gradual transition.
Consequently, the government, as in England and in
some countries on the Continent, assumes the cost of

maintenance and operation of denominational schools, in addition to that of public schools. This should be viewed, however, as an evolutionary step rather than a desirable end result. Were we to adopt a similar policy in the United States we should be turning back rather than going forward on the road of educational progress.

III

But what of the contention that fair play requires relief from double taxation? Let us not quibble about proportionate taxes. Can we justify, in fact, the necessity that Catholics lend support to both public and parochial school?

This takes us back to what was said a moment ago about education as a public responsibility. The state insists that children be afforded opportunities for education, and it rightfully taxes all citizens for this purpose. It does not require, however, that all children are to attend the public school. It permits parents to choose between education under public auspices and education under private auspices. Therefore, if this involves double taxation, it is nothing more than the normal consequence of the parents' decision. Quite properly, the state imposes as one condition for this freedom of choice that the resources available for public education be not diverted from their original object or weakened thereby! In short, it is one thing to grant the privilege of education under private auspices. It is another thing to expect the state to suffer the consequences of the exercise of this privilege.

The motives which prompt individuals to seek the

education of their children in non-public schools are legion. Some are worthy, others are short-sighted and limited. Some parents wish an opportunity through their children to explore new possibilities in education and, if successful, to contribute thereby to education in public as well as in private schools. Others seek out the private school as a special badge of privilege or to win for their children social and economic advantages not otherwise so easily attainable. Still others seek the special influences which a denominational institution alone can provide. Obviously the state cannot undertake to identify these motives within particular individuals or to sit in judgment upon them in order to discriminate between the schools that give expression to them. Nor does the fact that the creation of private schools helps to alleviate the burden of financing public education justify asking the public to assume the expense of private education. To adopt this principle would be to require the state to expend its resources on projects not of its own choosing.

At present only a few states lend direct support to sectarian schools. Nevertheless many Catholics and Protestants seek to induce the state to assume the burden of private education through subsidies for free textbooks and teaching materials, teachers' salaries, and the maintenance of buildings. To attain these ends they adopt the principle of one step at a time. Accordingly, pressure is at present exerted primarily on behalf of state assistance in providing transportation of children to and from school, health services, free textbooks and other instructional materials. In each instance the argument now used is that "it is the child which is aided, not the institution."

Obviously this is but a half-truth. To the extent that the cost of attendance in private schools is lessened for the individual, both the institution concerned and the child benefit therefrom. And since aid of this character to parochial schools depletes the funds available for public education, it hardly follows that the child alone is affected.

On the other hand, to provide health services free, and perhaps transportation as well, is different from furnishing free textbooks and instructional aids or underwriting the expense of teachers' salaries and building maintenance. Take health, for example. Not infrequently the state intervenes to protect the child from the misguided notions or the wilful neglect of his parents, in order to insure for him the primary conditions of healthy growth and development. That is to say, the state assumes both the right and the obligation to guarantee to each child the minimum essentials of health care. This it does because the health and physical well-being of the people are of general public concern. It seems to follow that children are entitled to receive health services irrespective of whether they attend a public or a non-public school or no school at all.

From this a helpful criterion emerges. There are some services to which each member of a community is entitled by virtue of his membership in that community. But these services should come to him directly from the public, not indirectly through subsidies to private organizations, unless the latter be the more economical and efficient method to employ. In other words, we should take literally the injunction that it is the child and not the institution which is to benefit. Unless this principle is followed honestly the state should adopt the alternative policy of insisting that non-public schools provide the essentials for health and physical fitness, just as in theory they must measure up to minimum standards of education, *as a condition for receiving a license to operate.* These are standard services which a school can rightly be required to assure its pupils as evidence of its ability to function as a school.

A similar principle applies to the free transportation of children by the public to and from school. Supplying free tickets for use on public conveyances by children, irrespective of the school they attend, is worthy of consideration; provided again, that the cost to the public of this transportation does not increase by virtue of the individual's decision to attend a non-public school. Expenses that follow from individual preferences should fall upon either the guardian of the child or the institution concerned, or both.

When we pass from the question of providing children in non-public schools with health services and free transportation, to the suggestion that the public likewise assume the cost of textbooks and instructional materials, teachers' salaries, and building maintenance, the problem changes character. Here the issue is clearly: "Shall the state finance private education?" And this brings us back to the point emphasized before. Shall the state, as represented in the public school system, officiate at its own funeral?

Thus far the decision of our people is in the negative. When the state of Oregon attempted to require by statute that the children of all citizens attend only public schools, the Supreme Court of the United States quite properly declared the act unconstitutional. Our country assures its people the choice of attending either the public school or a private school which meets certain basic educational requirements. Obviously, in so doing the public assumes certain risks. Private schools may influence children in ways inimical to the best interests of the state or inculcate ideas and dispositions altogether out of tune with the times. Nor is this danger purely theoretical. Private schools have perpetuated antiquated notions of the nature of man and the world. They have fomented unscientific doctrines of racial superiority and prejudices—religious, economic, and social—that run counter to the general welfare. Nevertheless Americans believe that the exercise of some freedom unwisely is less harmful in the long run than the imposition of conformity. In education as in other fields they believe with the late Justice Holmes that "the ultimate good desired is better reached by free trade in ideas" and that competition will in the end drive inferior practices out of existence. Consequently, they tolerate private education. But, once again, to permit parents to select a non-public school in which to educate their children in accordance with the religion of their convictions is one thing, and to expect the state to finance this choice is another. This limits the application of Wise's argument, when he writes:

"Catholics are morally obligated to secure a religious training for their children, and this does not mean religion separated from life, religion as a subject given during special and released time during the week or on Sundays, but religious

truths in literature, in philosophy, in history, not to speak
of other subjects." [13]

IV

Finally, we come to the argument that religious education, being indispensable for public welfare, merits
public support. As we saw in Chapter V, advocates of this
position draw an analogy between the practice of government aid to private enterprise in times of crisis and
the need to assist religious schools in distress. Government support is appropriate, it is argued, when an activity, manifestly essential for public welfare, cannot be
sustained wholly by private enterprise. Since this is obviously the case at present with respect to religious education, the state must hasten to the rescue.

In the light of the discussion in Chapter VI, I need not
dwell long on this argument. It assumes that one or another sectarian conception of religion underwrites
morality, whereas the fact seems to be that the spiritual
values men cherish in common are rooted in ways of
living which cut through sectarian differences and give
body to principles of conduct, even without benefit of
clergy. Now it is this social cement, in the form of character traits, the common virtues, and the values inherent
in democratic association—e.g., a respect for people as
persons, together with the disposition and will to realize
the best in oneself through fruitful and generous interrelationships with others—that are matters of public
concern. With respect to character education the state
cannot remain neutral. But *how* indispensable charac-

[13] *Ibid.*, p. 364.

teristics of personality and accepted moral principles are validated in a specific individual's philosophy or religion, is a matter upon which the state quite properly remains neutral. And since public education, given adequate support, can develop and maintain public schools that are amply qualified to educate for character and to imbue young people with the values of a democratic society, there is no need to drain the common treasury on behalf of sectarian interests.

But can the school in fact educate for character, without religion? How concretely can the secular school meet this supreme obligation? This, quite appropriately, is the concern of our concluding chapter.

Chapter IX

THE burden of the argument in previous chapters has been largely negative: to convince the reader that efforts to reintroduce religion into public education, while well-intentioned, are misguided. I have attempted to show that the reasons which prompt earnest men and women to demand religious instruction will not, of necessity, be satisfied thereby. The times are out of joint. Man's faith in man is severely challenged; crime and delinquency are on the increase in the younger age groups; established customs and habits no longer function smoothly; and economic dislocation generates fear and uncertainty. Under these conditions men crave security for themselves and their children and naïvely assume that if religious instruction were somehow added to the school curriculum, more stable influences would operate in the lives of their young.

Unfortunately the disease is not so easily cured. Many of the evils that beset us extend their roots deep down into the economic, social, and political order and are thus beyond the power of the school to correct. Others lie within the province of the school and can be attacked effectively; but religious instruction as such does not insure this outcome. More is called for than verbal instruction, whether it be religious or secular in character.

Moreover, I have argued that to introduce sectarian instruction into the schools may accentuate many of the difficulties we seek to eliminate. Instead of fostering the Christian spirit of tolerance, it tends to make children conscious of differences that, unfortunately, do not generate the spirit of peace and brotherly love. It likewise tends to perpetuate the false notion that the springs of conduct and of faith derive from the creeds that divide men rather than from the common stream of life, the basic cultural influences in which all share and to which each individual can make his own unique contribution.

There is no difference, however, between the advocates and the opponents of religion in public education regarding the need to use the school for character education and the development of spiritual values. As the authors of a significant volume on this problem put it:

"As over against the loss of faith, the perplexity, the spiritual unrest of many older people, the public school must upbuild in the young the spiritual values needed for a just and wholesome civilization. Instead of division and conflict, it must build unity. In place of doubt and fear it must build faith, faith in right and good, faith that effort wisely directed can in the long run prevail at least reasonably against the troubles that assail. Such a public service we . . . count the chief task and aim of the public school." [1]

As suggested in Chapter IV, this emphasis upon the spiritual mission of the school—spiritual in the sense of

[1] Brubacher and others, *The Public Schools and Spiritual Values*. New York: Harper & Brothers, 1944, p. 2.

helping young people to evolve ideals and standards with which to direct their lives—has been a major objective of educators for some years. The obvious limitations of mass education, together with the effects of the depression upon our youth, have challenged the school to reappraise its functions and to concern itself with the all-around needs of children and adolescents. Or, perhaps more accurately stated, the changing status of young people in American society in the past twenty-five years has stimulated educators ever more widely to realize in practice what John Dewey preached nearly fifty years ago. Writing in *The School and Society* at the close of the last century, Dewey described the manner in which a child—in the more nearly self-sustained home of that period—learned from participation in the essential tasks and activities of the home, from the conversations and discussions within the family circle, the workshop and the laboratory, which ideal parents would provide for him, and from his excursions into the larger world outside the home. "Now," concluded Dewey, "if we organize and generalize all this, we have the ideal school. There is no mystery about it, no wonderful discovery of pedagogy or educational theory. It is simply a question of doing systematically and in a large, intelligent and competent way what for various reasons can be done in most households only in a comparatively meager and haphazard manner." [2]

May we look more closely at these developments as reflected in the best schools of today?

[2] Chicago: The University of Chicago Press, 1900, pp. 50–51.

II

First is a greater preoccupation than formerly with the person-to-person relationship of the child, with the qualities of personality he comes to make his own from associations within the family, the school, and an ever widening community.

Concretely this means that guidance and education are closely identified. In contrast to the more exclusively academic emphasis of the traditional school, education now centers upon the child's healthy progress from immaturity toward maturity, upon his physical, emotional, social, and moral development, as well as, indeed, upon a condition of well-balanced intellectual growth.

This new approach is evident on the child's first day in school, that first crucial moment in his transition from the intimate family circle to the larger environment. The teacher's immediate objective is to help the child to feel at home, to sense the class group as an enlargement of the warm and intimate atmosphere of the family; and, conversely, to assist him to assume without undue strain the responsibilities that go with membership and to perform gladly the tasks essential for the ongoing life of the group, as a natural consequence of the fact that he is needed and wanted.

The teacher, in the role of a substitute parent, can render easy the transition from home to school, transforming what is often an unpleasant shock, with traumatic effects upon a child's personality, into a pleasing, even a thrilling experience. Here as elsewhere a good start is all-important. As the child moves on through the

elementary school he requires less detailed supervision
and direction. Indeed, the goal is an increasing degree
of independence and self-direction. However, this goal
is best achieved when the teacher realizes the possibilities of long-range as well as short-range guidance, and
recognizes that an all-important function of the school
in the person of the teacher is to further emotional and
social maturity as well as intellectual progress.

This process calls for a different emphasis at different
ages, since each stage of growth brings with it relatively
unique opportunities and problems. Adults need to re-
mind themselves of the fact that both the child and his
environment, as he senses it, undergo rapid transformations in relatively brief periods of time. Progress from
the nursery school age through the elementary school
and on into adolescence is a matter of rapidly changing
phases, a sequence of new impulses and interests in response to people and to things that, from the child's
viewpoint, refuse to remain pegged down. Basic to everything, however, is an abiding sense of security, a growing
self-assurance and confidence, that serves as an inner
citadel of defense against the normal casualties of life,
as well as a vantage point from which the young person
can venture forth hopefully and courageously into the
surrounding world. Given this sense of security, he has
little need to compensate for his lacks with tantalizing
characteristics of overaggressiveness, or undue submis-
siveness and docility, or inept and ineffectual demands
for affection, and with other evidences of maladjustment.
As his skills and his abilities mature, so does his capacity
for self-direction, and in the proportion that he becomes

an individual in his own right, he creates and deepens mutually stimulating channels of communication with his fellows.

Now, each of these stages of development gives character to the individual's *relationship* with people; and, be it observed, morality is a matter of relationships! For example, at the nursery age the child is self-centered and demanding. Only gradually does he find satisfaction in sharing with others and engaging in group play. However, as he moves into the elementary school, his interests tend more and more to embrace his associates. Soon the authority of the home finds supplementation and often a rival in the standards and the concerns of the clique and the gang. As one authority has stated:

"With this shift in authority comes a new attitude toward sex differences. In our society intense sex antagonism develops during these years, no matter how much we try to prevent it. Clubs and gangs exclude the opposite sex, and behavior toward the opposite sex is marked by a great deal of teasing. Whether this sex antagonism is part of normal psychological growth or a matter of cultural patterning is hard to determine." [3]

These characteristics do not persist, however. Hardly does the baffled parent or puzzled teacher learn how to cope with them than a new phase looms on the horizon:

"During the later terms of the elementary school period, children begin to shift from such intense interest in the group to marked preoccupation with one person of the same sex.

[3] Caroline B. Zachry, "Emotional Needs and Social Development," in *Elementary School Principals,* XV, No. 6 (July, 1936), pp. 262–263. Published by the Department of Elementary Principals of the National Education Association.

This attachment may take the form of a crush on an adult or
an older child; it may be worked out through hero worship
accompanied by a great deal of fantasy; or it may be manifested in a very absorbing friendship with a child of the same
age." [4]

Adolescence and the secondary school period mark a
further stage in which the young person begins to see
himself, other people, and the world in a new light. Lawrence K. Frank points out that adolescence, in our culture, frequently involves

"profound disturbances in the life of the individual, necessi-
tating unlearning much of what has been painfully acquired
in early childhood and accepting new beliefs and patterns of
conduct demanded of the individual for adult living. In our
culture, this involves emancipation from dependence upon
parental care and control in order to become more inde-
pendent and self-directing, in order to become an adult who
can live with one's contemporaries, accepting the responsibilities and opportunities of adult life. It also involves clarification and acceptance (or sometimes the rejection) of the
masculine and feminine roles, the development of relations
with members of the other sex which may arouse acute anx-
ieties because of the shame and guilt associated with genitals
and sex functions in early childhood. It also necessitates a
sometimes drastic reorganization of the child's picture of the
world and a reconsideration of all the phantasies and illusions about his parents, religion, government, business and
social life generally, with a concomitant alteration of the
image of the self." [5]

[4] *Ibid.*, p. 263.
[5] "The Emergence of Personality," *Transactions of The New York
Academy of Sciences,* Series II, Vol. VI, No. 5 (March, 1944), p. 154.

Need I remark that the growing pains associated with the various stages in childhood and adolescence are not confined to the young person? Rare indeed is the parent who can keep pace with his child. Particularly in late childhood and adolescence does the maturity of the young person exceed the expectations of his parents. The understanding that leads to skill and ingenuity in providing the appropriate environment for each phase of growth, and the humor and the endurance that are requisite to prevent older people from kicking too vigorously against the pricks, constitute invaluable assets for parent and teacher alike; and, obviously, they bear on the ease with which the child himself progresses from step to step.

It is here that the school can help, not only in providing the situations and the materials requisite for healthy growth, but also in supplementing the home and the psychological insight of the parent. Neither the home nor the school can wisely function in isolation. In many schools conferences are held with parents on the admission of the child to the school, so that the teacher may know at once the status of the child in the home—the nature of the parent-child relationship, the number of the children in the home, the way in which the child adjusts to brothers and sisters and they to him—all with a view to furthering continuity of experience and enabling both school and home the better to marshal their respective resources.

Group conferences with parents are likewise important; they evolve often into study groups, supplemented by individual conferences so that the general principles developed can be applied to the specific problem of Johnny and Mary. Fortunately, materials on all aspects of child care are now available in nontechnical language. Organizations such as the Child Study Association of America, the National Committee on Mental Hygiene, the Children's Bureau in Washington, and a number of other lay and professional groups, have published a wealth of information pertaining to all aspects of child development, from feeding and clothing to the nature of the discipline and direction of behavior which are best calculated to yield in children desirable qualities of personality. Moreover, the education of teachers today includes a training designed to render them skillful in detecting crucial symptoms of growth, both healthy and unhealthy, so that to their competence in their own classrooms can be added assistance to the home. Not infrequently the tactful teacher, in the process of helping parents to provide wisely for the child in his activities and his relations within the home, exercises a profound influence upon all members of the family.

Nor is parent education an exclusive concern of the nursery school and primary grades. Each succeeding phase of child development challenges parent and school anew. Each period brings its unique opportunities and its problems. To capitalize fully on the assets involves the constant utilization of new resources, materials, and activities. For example, in the early years and, by and large, throughout the elementary school period, children long for a manifest interest on the part of their parents in their work at school. This longing enables the school, if it will, to create an intimate community in which par-

ents and teachers and children each play an appropriate·
role. Ere long, however, and clearly by the time the pupil reaches the upper years of high school, parental guidance is best exercised at a respectful distance. In these
years there is a demand for cultivation within the community of resources not only for healthy recreation but
also for social and economic education.

I have dwelt at some length upon the guidance function of the school in order to emphasize that life within
the school lends itself to the development of qualities in
children, parents, and teachers alike which make for
intelligent and responsive citizenship. Good schools
realize this fact and organize classroom, extracurricular
activity, and relations with the home accordingly.

Consider, for example, the school in its associations
with parents. This function of the school illustrates the
motto, "In union there is strength." By bringing together
parents of a class group or of the entire school, the school
both supplements and reinforces its own labors. Often
the existence of a parents' association enables the school
to solve problems of the community that previously de-
fied solution. Parents' associations frequently not only
agree upon rules and regulations governing social relations outside the school, but also constitute mutual aid
societies in devising constructive things to do with their
children. By helping parents to answer the question,
"What shall I do with my child at home, in order to live
fruitfully with him?" or, "How can I employ his time
profitably in home and neighborhood?" the school, either
directly or, better, indirectly through the co-operative
activities of the parents' organization, contributes to the

moral well-being of children. Likewise through group discussion and courses of study, parents' organizations can improve parents' understanding of the needs of children or can suggest how they can minister constructively to these needs; while, in the way in which the school itself encourages children to live and work together in the school, it determines what habits and codes and ideals they will make their own.

President Day of Cornell University once remarked that for many children the school affords the only opportunity to acquire the basic social habits, since most homes lack the facilities essential for their continued practice. Be this as it may, it is certainly true that the good school can develop through practice as well as precept both the basic moral principles of a democracy and the habits and virtues which constitute the indispensable social cement of a civilized society.

Nor is this a responsibility the school can safely delegate to others, although it naturally shares with the home, the church, and other agencies a common obligation to children. No institution, other than the home, can perform so well what modern educators conceive to be the unique function of the school. Nor do many parents possess at present the training which enables them to comprehend fully the needs of children and adolescents, or to provide constructively for these needs. Consequently it is the school's unique task to bring to bear upon young people the influences requisite for all-around development; to remedy defects and maladjustments of personality when its resources permit; to suggest or to enlist the help of specialists when these are called for; and to engage the large body of normal children in work and play designed to produce free and effective personalities.

There is no occasion for segregating pupils into classes on religion in order to achieve these objectives!

III

A second characteristic of the modern school is implicit in what I have said about guidance and education. Learning is no longer conceived solely in intellectual terms. Verbal education has its place, indeed an indispensable place, since relations with the far away and the long ago and communication at long distance are far more necessary today than they were some generations back. But words are symbols, and to concentrate upon words and intellectual response alone is to deal with the surface of life. The moral for much of our teaching today is summed up nicely in the following statement:

"Teaching exists to foster and promote learning. And the young learn what they live. Hence, teaching in order to foster learning must foster living, the kind of living fit to be learned and built into character." [6]

This emphasis upon learning as living and upon the kind of living that fosters learning leads to a revolution in school procedure. Only when superficially interpreted has it encouraged a neglect of the past, since obviously the past can throw light upon the full significance of the present. At times, when applied without reference to child psychology or without an understanding

[6] Brubacher and others, *op. cit.*, p. 110.

of the characteristics and potentialities of children at different ages, it has resulted in unwise and overly mature involvement of children in the problems and the controversies of adult society. Nevertheless, the recognition that children learn what they live has directed attention generally in schools (1) to forces actually operating within children's lives as potential grist for the mills of education, and (2) to the devising of experiences that offset serious undernourishments in home and community.

May I illustrate with respect to education for social responsibility?

The recent war brought home to educators opportunities for service within the schools which previously had been neglected. Often a plain necessity of supplementing the work of the janitor or the cleaner rendered easy the introduction of work experience. In one school, by no means an exception to the rule,

"the older children have undertaken to assist in the care of younger children during rest periods and meal hours. In addition, they help to care for rooms, build furniture and equipment for the kindergarten, and devote art periods to the illustration of stories and nursery rhymes for the very young. Out of this has come not merely an intimate acquaintance between age groups, a fellowship, or better, a family atmosphere hitherto absent in the school, but as well a stabilizing emotional influence upon the older children themselves. The work of the school is no less interesting. The child with an art, a shop, or a science or food interest can still use this interest to better his knowledge and his skill; but, more, he grounds it firmly and gives it objective validity by virtue of the fact that by means of it he furthers the life of his com-

munity. To the surprise of the shop teachers in this institution, the sixth grade boys, who devoted their shop periods to
the construction of furniture for the kindergarten, were not
only as keenly interested in their work as formerly, but they
more willingly held themselves to a high level of performance. They employed an effective and objective standard for
good work and were freed from the temptation to conclude
at a critical moment 'Well, anyway, that is good enough for
me.'

"Of chief importance, in this instance, is the quality of
relationships fostered by these new departures. The older
children no longer look upon the very young child as a nui-
sance and a pest. Nor is the older child an indifferent or an
unsympathetic stranger to the young. A good family atmosphere pervades the school and genuine affection has grown
up between big and little. Moreover, service experiences yield
grist for discussions on the part of older children in which the
behavior traits of the small child are made known and thus,
indirectly, the older children acquire an insight into their
own behavior in relation to their brothers and sisters. Parents report less tension and improved relationships within
their homes." [7]

Contact with the community outside the school is
particularly valuable for adolescents. The adolescent
craves an opportunity to function as an adult, and to
perform services which adults recognize as important.
Nor is importance measured for him solely in vocational
terms, although a potential or an actual job is closely
associated in a young person's mind with the right to
stand on his own feet and to make his own decisions.

[7] V. T. Thayer, *American Education Under Fire*. New York and
London: Harper & Brothers, 1944, pp. 171–172.

Civic interests are also potent at this age and social service projects that are fruitful in fostering social maturity and stable qualities of personality. Here too the school can help by devising ways and means of relating students through their interests to the larger community:

"Thus the art student, as an integral part of his development as an artist, can study and perhaps contribute toward meeting the art needs of the community. Similarly the science student can assist in a hospital or a health clinic or perhaps in a municipal health department where scientific principles receive application. He thus acquires a sense of reality not otherwise possible and the numerous possibilities of science as a vocational and a civic contribution become manifest to him.

"Recently a class group in a secondary school conducted a survey of the immediate community in which the school is located. In the course of their investigation they discovered a number of mothers of poor families who were unable to supplement the family income because of the need to remain home with their children. After deliberating upon the situation, the class decided to appeal to the student body in support of the establishment of a day nursery. The girls volunteered to assist a trained worker in the nursery, and to acquire the essentials of child care thus involved; other students helped to equip it. In short, out of a classroom study, blossomed a social-civic project which gave first-hand assurance to the students that they could play a significant role in their community along the lines of a major interest of the school." [8]

In recent years secondary schools have come to realize the educational values in "work-service" programs. Not merely the obvious advantages that emerge from a job

[8] *Ibid.,* p. 172.

for which the boy or girl receives pay, but also from work given without pay in order to meet a need in a community or a social agency that might otherwise not be met. Here again the war revealed opportunities at hand not fully appreciated previously. Hospitals, settlements, day care centers, public libraries, and numerous other agencies both public and private now receive assistance from students in secondary schools. In one school a joint faculty-student committee was created to search out, register, and assign jobs that needed doing, not merely in the course of the school year but in the summer months as well. The rapid development of the summer work camp, which provides both work for pay and a free will contribution to worthy causes, illustrates the eagerness of young people to devote themselves to tasks that challenge their powers and bear witness to their worth. Observers of work experience for young people of high school age are impressed with the maturing effects of socially significant work. They say it engenders a healthy self-respect, constitutes an excellent foundation for economic and social understanding, provides the discipline that comes from seeing a job through because of its manifest importance, fosters the spirit of co-operation, and, particularly in the summer work camp, gives an invaluable experience in democratic living.[9]

[9] *The School Executive* for August 1945 contains an excellent series of articles dealing with work experience, which are reprinted and distributed by the School Executive and Associated Junior Work Camps, Inc., 442 West 238th Street, New York City. See also "Work Experience," published by the American Education Fellowship, 289 Fourth Avenue, New York City. An excellent review of the place of work in secondary education, prepared by Warren C. Seyfert and entitled "Providing Work and Service Experience for Postwar Youth," appears in the *Twenty-Fourth Yearbook*, Part I, National Society for the Study of Education, University of Chicago Press, Chicago, Ill., 1945.

It is by direct experience that schools give body to the basic moral principles implicit in democracy, such as respect for personality and the brotherhood of man. These principles are best exemplified in practice so that later, when formulated as ideals, they will still have blood in their veins.

Nor do schools lack occasion to give a present meaning to the democratic ideal of the worth of people, the principle that people are persons and should receive treatment as such. Attempts to offset racial and religious antagonism and discrimination begin appropriately in the school itself. A heterogeneous school population and a heterogeneous faculty constitute natural soil in which to plant seeds of tolerance and an active acceptance of the idea that people are persons.

How a respect for people and their backgrounds may be acquired in school is clearly exemplified in the widely known work of Springfield, Massachusetts. As Alland and Wise state in their able and interesting birds-eye view of school and community activities in Springfield:

"The indifferences of children to differences in race or color, unless these are forcibly brought to attention, is attested by the incident concerning the class shown here. [A picture of a colored teacher and her class.] Some parents were surprised to learn, on visiting the school, that this teacher was a Negro. So unimportant had that fact seemed to the children, almost all of whom were white, that at home they had merely said they liked their arithmetic teacher, without mentioning the fact that she happened to be colored.

"Similar acceptance of Irish, French, Jewish, and Polish teachers by classes which are predominantly of other national backgrounds has become axiomatic through the Springfield

schools. The over-all program which accentuates personal
worth and eliminates spurious judgments along racial and
religious lines has made this not only possible but inevitable.

"Moreover, the acceptance of differences in the classroom
and on the playground carries over into the attitudes which
the children take back to their homes. The resulting uncon-
scious re-education of parents by children is not the least of
the benefits to be derived in the process of living together as
equals." [10]

More and more schools realize that the way of life
which prevails in the classroom, on the playground,
and in extracurricular activity is all-important in determining attitudes and dispositions and, ultimately,
ideals. Consequently authoritarian motives of discipline
and school organization are giving way to democratic
relationships. For a time the reaction against the old
confused teachers and children alike. Chaos, however,
was short-lived, and most schools now sense the fact that
preparation for a free society requires guidance, not license, and that young people will become progressively
self-directive when they participate in plans and activities appropriate to their maturity. Life in the elementary and secondary school now encourages thinking and
planning in advance of action; and out of this thinking
and planning emerge the criteria which children gladly
employ because they have shared in their formulation.

A squabble on the playground or a dispute over the
use of a tool in the shop is no longer settled by an arbitrary act of the instructor in charge. Occasion is taken

[10] *The Springfield Plan*, photographs by Alexander Alland, text by
James Waterman Wise. New York: Viking Press, 1945, pp. 50–51.

to talk the problem out, perhaps with the entire class group. From discussion emerges an understanding not only of the rules that must obtain if each person is to enjoy his rights, but of why one way of settling a difficulty is better than another. Decisions of this character tend to establish two principles basic to a democracy: the right of each individual to a hearing and to his "fair share" in the resources of the group, and the necessity that each member of a community adjust his wants and his claims to the needs of others.

Not only does the school provide a wealth of individual occasions in which to develop social ideals; it is itself a social institution which students can study with profit. Of this I have elsewhere said:

"If the life of the school may be used to provide experience for developing social insight and responsibility, it may also serve as a miniature community for the laboratory study of the patterns and motives of social organization. Each department of the school may not only make its own contribution to the life of the school; it may also use the life of the school as legitimate subject-matter for its own work.

"At present the social-studies department is most obviously in a position to use the institutional life of the school in this way. For example, the editorial board of a high-school paper confronts in small the social problem of competition and profit in its advertising policy: shall it assume responsibility for the influence of its advertisements upon the readers of the paper, or shall it subscribe to the doctrine, 'Read at your own risk'? In choices like these, faculty and students select the motives that will continue to operate in the future, and situations of this sort are eminently valuable for analysis in the social-studies class.

"The operations of a student-government organization are also excellent grist for the mill of the social-studies teacher. The management of student affairs constantly gives rise to issues that cut deep into the foundations of political economy. On one occasion a student organization was attempting to elect officers for the ensuing year. A wave of negativism swept through the student body, and all individuals nominated for office refused to stand for election. The instructor of a civics class used this situation as an opportunity to explore the responsibility of the individual in relation to civic activities and enterprises. The motives and responsibilities of participants in student government and those of citizens in municipal, state, and national affairs were contrasted and the bearing of political habits on citizenship examined.

"In most secondary schools and colleges the demand to reorganize the student government arises at periodic intervals, practically once in each student generation. Instructors can use this opportunity to help young people sense the fact that forms of government are instruments created to accomplish common purposes, and that, since these purposes reflect both the needs and the personalities of individuals, governmental forms are likely to undergo change when one generation is replaced by another. Students may thus profitably inquire into the ways in which events in the school are duplicated on a larger and more complicated scale in municipal, state, and national affairs.

"And so to greater or less extent with other departments of the school. Each may study the group life of the school community from the vantage point of its own subject-matter. Each may draw relevant conclusions about the life of the larger community of which the school is but a fragment. Surveys of art in the school (lighting and decoration), of student opinion, of the factors influencing choice of items on the menu of the school cafeteria, of transportation problems of

THE SCHOOL AND CHARACTER EDUCATION 183

students and faculty, of library facilities, of numbers and types of student organizations—these and others come readily to mind as examples.

"This kind of analysis of the integrated community life of the school is comparatively objective and intellectual. As such it serves a purpose somewhat distinct from that of acquiring social attitudes and devotion to group aims through participation in the school community, discussed above. It is designed to establish the habit and the ability to look objectively at the group life in which one participates, and to study that group life for its wider social implications. Hence it leads directly toward a closer scrutiny of the wider groups in which the student is involved outside the relatively immediate environment of his schooling."[11]

The skillful teacher thus relates talk and action in order to "teach" the virtues, knowing full well that the vitality of the one derives from association with the other. And since, as we have seen, the daily life of the school provides numerous occasions for these two ways of learning to reinforce each other, it is a medium supremely important for character building. Here again the war and the challenge which the Nazis hurled at the democracies to justify the principles they would live by, have exercised a profound influence upon education. Educators recognize as never before the need to make explicit the values they would have young people make their own. The worth of the individual; the idea that conflicting programs of living are to be thought out and talked out—in the hope that thought and discussion will gen-

[11] *Reorganizing Secondary Education*, by V. T. Thayer, Caroline B. Zachry, and Ruth Kotinsky. New York: D. Appleton-Century Co., 1939, pp. 212–213.

erate a workable solution—rather than fought out; the
fact that men realize their best possibilities when the self-
expression of one becomes a means for the self-realization
of another—these are no longer pious expressions. They
are as a cloud by day and a pillar of fire by night.[12]

IV

The necessity of making explicit the values we live by
and of meeting more adequately than formerly the needs
of young people has also changed the purpose to which
subject matter is put in schools of today. Publications of
the Educational Policies Commission and of the Commission on the Secondary School Curriculum of the
Progressive Education Association amply illustrate this
point.[13] Taken together they constitute a well-stocked

[12] For an abundance of illustrations of ways in which schools are giving young people an opportunity to live democratically, see *Learning
the Ways of Democracy*, Educational Policies Commission, Washington,
D.C., 1940.

[13] Publications of the Educational Policies Commission of the National
Education Association, Washington, D.C.:

The Unique Function of Education in American Democracy, 1937;
The Purposes of Education in American Democracy, 1938; *The Structure
and Administration of Education in American Democracy*, 1938; *Learning the Ways of Democracy, a Case Book in Civic Education*, 1940; *The
Education of Free Men in American Democracy*, 1941.

Publications of the Commission on the Secondary School Curriculum
are published by D. Appleton-Century Co., New York City. These are as
follows:

Reorganizing Secondary Education, by V. T. Thayer, Caroline B.
Zachry, and Ruth Kotinsky; *Art in General Education*, by the Committee
on the Function of Art in General Education; *Language in General Edu-
cation*, by the Committee on the Function of English in General Educa-
tion; *Mathematics in General Education*, by the Committee on Mathematics in General Education; *Science in General Education*, by the Committee on Science in General Education; *The Social Studies in General
Education*, by the Committee on the Social Studies in General Education; *Teaching Creative Writing*, by Lawrence H. Conrad; *Prose Fiction*

library of practical suggestions for virtually every department of the school. Volumes of the Commission on the Secondary School Curriculum are particularly helpful, since they were written by committees consisting of teachers, administrators, research workers, and students of adolescent development. They grew out of work actually being done in schools and they point the way to further reorganization of schools in response to the growing pains of young people and the ideals of a democratic society.

Take, for example, the report on *Science in General Education*. This report calls attention to the needs of adolescents as they grow up in our society, conceiving "needs" as being at once personal and social in nature; as resulting from "interactions between the individual and the social situation"; and as the outcome of "a want [biological tension] or a desire on the one hand, and the requirements, demands, standards of social living on the other." The report describes four large areas of needs, thus viewed, that properly become the concern of science teachers in secondary schools: needs of Personal Living, of Immediate Personal-Social Relationship, of Social-Civic Relationship, and of Economic Relationship. Since, moreover, democracy places a premium upon certain characteristics of personality—such as social sensitivity, tolerance, co-operativeness, the disposition to use reflective thinking in the solution of problems, creative-

---

in General Education: Bibliographies of 1,500 Novels Selected, Classified, and Annotated for Use in Meeting the Needs of Students in Senior High School and Junior College, by Elbert Lenrow. See also *Emotion and Conduct in Adolescence,* by Caroline B. Zachry, and *The Adolescent Personality,* by Peter Blos.

ness, self-direction, aesthetic appreciation—the authors are not content merely to reveal the resources of science as subject matter which can minister to the needs of youth. They go to great pains to illustrate in detail the procedure and the methods which teachers can employ in order to help young people to acquire these desirable traits of personality. Subject matter and method are thus viewed not as ends in themselves but as means for realizing the goals of a democratic education.

Studies in literature, the social studies, art, mathematics follow a similar plan. Stimulated by this pioneer work, curriculum committees in a goodly number of states and in innumerable cities and towns have undertaken a like task with reference to the peculiar conditions obtaining in their own localities. No one who reviews these studies can rightfully accuse public schools of indifference to character development. On the contrary, an earnest desire to create conditions favorable to growth, in ways consistent with democratic ideals, is a distinctive characteristic of curricular reform of recent years on all levels of education—elementary, secondary, and college.

A reversion to religious instruction at this time might very well defeat or divert these efforts. It would encourage the school to delegate to others the responsibility which it is admirably qualified to discharge: the cultivation of common ideals, standards, and ways of living in young people who differ in religion, race, nationality and social-economic status.

This does not mean that religion is to remain unmentioned in the school. On the contrary, *in a context ap-*

propriate to the public school it is present in virtually every good school.

What is this context?

It is, for one thing, the use of religion for acquainting young people with the cultural groups and forces within their own community, for developing in them an appreciation and a sympathetic understanding of the people with whom they associate daily and the background out of which they come—in short, for purposes of education, not propaganda.

Springfield, Massachusetts, again furnishes us with a happy illustration. In the eighth grade at Springfield, the children engage in the study of changing civilizations. This introduces them naturally to the great religions of history and the influence of these religions upon the political and economic life of people. From the study of the effect of religion upon India, for example, the pupils are prompted to investigate its influence upon other countries. In each case they can glean evidence of both the contributions and the limitations of the particular religion under investigation. It is helpful, for instance, to discover the principles of morality and attitudes of man toward man that permeate the great religions, as well as the exceptions to this rule. As one observer remarks of a class in Springfield:

"One class made a model of a ship's wheel, symbol of guidance, and wrote upon each spoke a statement of the Golden Rule from a different religion. Several of the children testified that they had acquired from these facts an increased respect for all religions, including their own." [14]

14 *The Story of the Springfield Plan*, by Clarence I. Chatto and Alice L. Halligan. New York: Barnes & Noble, 1945, p. 73.

Knowledge about religion finds a natural and proper place in the school curriculum from the earliest years. In both the primary and the elementary school children manifest a friendly attitude toward the strange and the different. This is a happy time at which to introduce the customs and the ways of people in other times and places. Nor is this introduction confined to verbal experience. Arts and crafts, dramatic work and music, give an emotional and aesthetic quality to what is learned. If to this is added later a study of the racial and national groups which compose our own population, children are helped to catch a vision of America as truly a melting pot, in which the contributions of many races, religions, and national characteristics are conserved and blended into one common life.

When the study of religion serves the sole purpose of intercultural education, and when its emphasis is on mutual understanding of groups, it is possible to enlist the interest and co-operation of representatives of the various religious organizations in the community. Chatto and Halligan write in this connection:

"A certain amount of opposition to the study of religions, even historically, in the public schools was expected, but the unit brought no word of hostile criticism. On the contrary, many favorable comments were received from parents who had themselves become interested in the study and through their children had co-operated on it. Clergymen of different faiths were consulted in the construction of the unit, both individually and in group conferences. Protestant, Roman Catholic, and Jewish teachers made invaluable contributions not only in ideas, but also in providing opportunities for pupils to learn through observation and experience. At the request of a number of her pupils, a Jewish teacher took them to the services at her synagogue and explained the meaning of what they saw. Through the help of a Catholic teacher, an interfaith group attended mass at the Roman Catholic cathedral and afterwards visited at the rectory, where the service was explained to them." [15]

The study *about* religion likewise occurs naturally in the social studies, on the high school and the college level. A typical illustration is taken from *Intercultural Education News*. The tenth-grade World History in Chevy Chase, Maryland, is organized on the basis of Institutions, of which, of course, religion is one.

"The large understanding sought under this topic is, 'How do the various religions of the world characterize the culture that gave rise to them?' Some of the problems studied are: Why man has developed religion, religious customs which have persisted, how the church became a guardian of standards, and how other religions than Christianity have spread ideals of living. Using this framework as a background, it is not difficult for the pupils to find many opportunities to understand and appreciate other religious groups. They see how in all religions man has attempted to find the answers to questions which determine his way of life. They understand how many religious customs have persisted even after the reason for them has ceased to be. The students also learn how the religions have contributed to one another. Pupils report on their own religions and explain to the class some of the local church practices. One unit such as this cannot change unsocial attitudes which have developed over a period of years and which very often are fostered by the home, but it

15 *Ibid.*, p. 72.

is a beginning. It gives the pupils something to think about, and it gives them facts with which to answer remarks heard outside of school. As one girl put it, 'The things "they" do, do not seem to be so "dumb" now.' " [16]

I have stressed knowledge about religion as an appropriate function of the school, in order to identify clearly the line beyond which it is neither wise nor necessary to go. Few teachers are competent to subject the creedal aspects of religion to the sifting and winnowing process of critical inquiry. Nor would many, if any, communities tolerate such an attempt of the school. Professor John Childs wisely comments on this point:

"Whenever and wherever the leaders and adherents of the various churches agree that the creeds and the rival claims and practices of religion can be studied by the ordinary, empirical procedures characteristic of the other work of the public school, little difficulty will be experienced in making a study of these aspects of religion also a part of the program of public education. Until that more ideal situation is reached in the religious life of the country, the present working arrangement is likely to be continued." [17]

Were there less effort by the partisans of religion to force the Bible upon the schools for purposes of religious instruction, there would be little objection to its use as one of the "great books," and, incidentally, as a source of moral wisdom. Indeed to exclude any great piece of literature from the schools (granted that it is appropriate

[16] Reported by Dorothy L. Gottschall, in *Intercultural Education News.* New York: Bureau for Intercultural Education, III, No. 4 (June, 1945), p. 5.
[17] Brubacher and others, *op. cit.,* p. 78.

to the age level) is reprehensible—provided, again, that we have in mind education and not propaganda.

Schools which teach Ethics to heterogeneous groups find the Bible and other sacred literature invaluable. In the Ethical Culture Schools of New York City, for example, Ethics has been an inherent part of the curriculum for several generations. As such it is not an isolated subject. Rather it is an opportunity for an understanding teacher to help children to interpret their on-going experience, by examining this experience, and talking out problems and confusions in a calm, objective, and friendly atmosphere.

I am appending to this chapter extracts from a course of study in Ethics, as taught in the elementary grades of the Ethical Culture Schools. These extracts illustrate not only ways in which the Bible and other literary material may be used to help children gain insight into relationships with parents and siblings and classmates, but also a suggestive substitute for religious instruction.

V

Finally, I return to the unique function of the public school which was briefly discussed in Chapter VII. I refer to the obligation of public education to discipline the mind. Education, as the Nazis practiced it, should bring home to everyone in a democracy the tragic consequences that follow when schooling is used to form the minds of the young rather than to encourage their development. Democracy and authoritarian education cannot go hand in hand, since democracies look to the people to render critical decisions. But the people can decide the issues of life wisely only as they are trained in the methods of reliable thought.

This places a heavy responsibility upon the school, and one, incidentally, that it has not carried long. Schooling is still identified in the minds of many with the acquisition of knowledge, or better, information, and with the passive reception of truths already salted down. This accounts for the respect or the fear commonly accorded the printed page. People find it hard to realize that reading need not mean believing and that thinking tends to become uncritical unless it is challenged. Consequently they object when a school library subscribes to magazines, or contains books, with which they disagree; and they are even more uneasy when a teacher deals at first hand with controversial issues in the classroom.

Gradually, however, the profession of teaching has become a distinctive function in a free society: to equip the minds of the young to earn and to preserve their freedom by acquiring the art and the science of thinking. Toward this end the teaching of virtually every subject in the school curriculum is undergoing reconstruction, so that each is gradually shedding its dogmatic and authoritarian character and serving better its potential functions in the development of intelligence.

John Dewey remarked several years ago that "the spirit in which the sciences are taught, and the methods of instruction employed in teaching them, have been in large measure taken over from traditional non-scientific subjects." [18] He meant that science teachers were failing

---

[18] *International Encyclopedia of Unified Science*, I, No. 1 (July, 1938), p. 36 (University of Chicago Press).

to develop understanding and use of scientific procedure. "There may be laboratories," he states, "and laboratory exercises and yet this statement remains true. For they may be employed primarily in order that pupils acquire a certain body of information. The resulting body of information about facts and laws has a different content from that provided in other studies. But as long as the ideal is information, the sciences taught are still under the domination of ideas and practices that have a pre-scientific origin and history." [19]

One of the contributions of progressive education has been to substitute pupil investigation for the old-fashioned recitation from a text. Children in the modern school are encouraged to seek answers to their own questions and to refine their procedures in the process, to use the laboratory for purposes other than a mere rehearsal of experiments previously performed, and to acquire at least the rudimentary methods of research by consulting libraries and original source materials, conducting interviews, going on excursions, etc. Recently the children of a third grade class in elementary science added to their knowledge of anatomy by dissecting a chicken. After the fowl had been completely taken apart, organ from organ and bone from bone, one child suggested that the skeleton be put together again. Patiently the class labored at the task, and successfully, with the exception of one last bone which seemed permanently to have lost its home. The children advanced several theories as to the bone's rightful location, but in each case trial revealed at least a debatable doubt. Soon the

[19] *Ibid.*, p. 36.

class was divided into rival groups, each convinced that the other was wrong. As the science period neared its conclusion a solution of the problem became pressing. Suspense and uncertainty were distressing. Finally, one child suggested that the correct location be decided upon by vote!

Here was an opportunity, fortunately seized upon by the teacher, to reveal to the children that not all questions lends themselves to decision by majority vote; that, indeed, some solutions are altogether irrelevant to human wishes. Later, as these children progress through school they will be introduced, if well taught, to the techniques of effective thinking: the exact logic characteristic of mathematics, the controlled methods of investigation peculiar to the natural sciences, the somewhat different procedures of the social scientist, and the still different manner in which men resolve conflicts between values. They will also learn that the context in which problems arise determines to what extent one or more of these methods is relevant or appropriate. And should they go farther and study the history of thought, they will observe that a close relationship obtains between its emancipation from authoritarian control and the steady refinement of objective and disinterested methods of inquiry on the one hand, and between the emancipation of the people from external and arbitrary control and the steady growth of democracy on the other.

It is this close relationship between democracy and untrammeled inquiry that gives importance to training in effective thinking in public education.

Nor is there anything inconsistent between this emphasis upon free inquiry and the methods of character education outlined in this chapter. But there is a contradiction and an inconsistency between the methods of instruction which constitute the peculiar responsibility of the school and instruction in religion in classes that are segregated for the purpose of winning adherents to a particular faith. This is not to say that parents or others outside the school should not employ methods of persuasion intended primarily to enlist conviction. Not even a school man will insist that educational methods must dominate the whole of life! My contention is rather that religious views, essentially private and sectarian, are inappropriately taught within the public school.

Nearly forty years ago John Dewey recognized this inconsistency between the spirit of education in schools and the special interests of religious instruction. Said he:

"Already the spirit of our schooling is permeated with the feeling that every subject, every topic, every fact, every professed truth must submit to a certain publicity and impartiality. All proffered samples of learning must go to the assay-room and be subjected to common tests. It is the essence of all dogmatic faiths to hold that any such 'show-down' is sacrilegious and perverse. . . . What is to be done about this increasing antinomy between the standard for coming to know in other subjects of the school and coming to know in religious matters? I am far from saying that the antinomy is an inherent one, or that the day may not come when religion will be so thoroughly naturalized in the hearts and minds of men that it can be considered publicly, openly, and by common tests, even among religious people. But it is pertinent to point out that, as long as religion is conceived as it now is conceived by the great majority of professed religionists, there is something self-contradictory in speaking of education in religion in the same sense in which we speak of education in topics where the method of free inquiry has made its way. The 'religious' would be the last to be willing that either the history or the content of religion should be taught in this spirit; while those to whom the scientific standpoint is not a merely technical device, but is the embodiment of integrity of mind, must protest against its being taught in any other spirit." [20]

VI

The purpose of this chapter was to answer the question, "Can the school educate for character by means of its own resources, or must it supplement these resources by means of religious instruction?" In reply I have attempted to document a twofold conclusion: first, that character education, broadly conceived, has become the central concern of modern education, and, second, that the resources now available to public school teachers lend themselves specifically to this task. Consequently, to attempt to supplement the public school by means of religious instruction will tend to distract attention from its truly great possibilities and weaken its effectiveness.

In supporting the thesis that schools are primarily concerned with character education, I pointed to the tendency today to conceive of the primary and elementary school as an extension of the home, or, if we will, as an enlarged home pervaded with a spirit of warmth and intimacy and presided over by an understanding teacher. This teacher organizes life within the classroom with an

[20] From "Religion and Our Schools," in *The Hibbert Journal* for July, 1908. Reprinted in *John Dewey's Philosophy,* edited, with an introduction, by Joseph Ratner. New York: The Modern Library, 1939, p. 711.

eye to the constructive development of the child's personality. Materials and activities, work and play, all serve this end; and, in order to give consistency and continuity to the child's development, mutually helpful relations between the home and the school are encouraged. Secondly, I mentioned the conception of learning that has come to dominate education, the realization that we learn what we live and live what we learn. The implications of this fact explain the shift in emphasis in education from the passive absorption of information and the docile acquisition of skills and techniques, to the creation of a suitable environment in which young people can participate actively. Schools are becoming communities and increasingly they afford young people the opportunity to do and to study things relevant to their growing needs and the needs of the society in which they live. In line with these trends efforts are made to involve children and adolescents in tasks that develop both personal and social habits and ideals. In the performance of these tasks, it is hoped, young people will acquire both a sense of security, an assurance that they are wanted and needed, and a feeling of identification with worthy causes larger than themselves. Third, I referred briefly, all too briefly, to recent trends in the reorganization of courses of study and curricula in schools. These changes are reflecting themselves in textbooks and methods and procedures in the classrooms. Outstanding in these developments is the attempt to see the world through the eyes of young people—to understand the questions they ask, the problems and confusions that beset them, and also their fundamental hopes and aspirations. These needs of children and adolescents are, of course, the result of the interplay between the individual and his world, and they can be met adequately only when the demands of society, broadly and wisely conceived, are understood in their impact upon youth. Much remains to be done before education has succeeded fully in exploiting the possibilities of this approach—but its implications and its promise for character education are clear. Finally, I drew attention to the unique responsibility of the school in preparing young people for intelligent participation in a free society, a society that is constantly changing and daily confronting its citizens with new and unsolved problems. Since these citizens must themselves arrive at decisions, schools are charged with training young people in the methods of thinking, and in ways of resolving conflicts in interests, that are both honest and objective. The dictum, "Ye shall know the truth and the truth shall make ye free" applies only when we have learned the ways of truth-seeking.

A cynical rebuttal of what I have outlined would be to say, "Show me the school that accomplishes these things."

I am frank to admit that few schools succeed as well as we might wish. But the moral is not to weaken them further or to divert them from their manifest responsibility. The penalty of so doing might well be tragic for American democracy. No, the course to follow is to further these obvious tendencies in modern education by insisting that schools realize ever more adequately their responsibilities to the communities they serve. Are we genuinely concerned with the welfare of our children and the upbuilding and the safeguarding of our democracy? If so, let us see to it that the school fulfills its sacred obligation to the young people and to the society of which they are members.

The American school is a unique institution. In a very real sense it has become a substitute for the American frontier. Free education enables each generation to acquire something akin to a new start in life. The free school is a place in which the children of all the people can meet under conditions as nearly equal as human frailty permits. The American school is also unique in that it is equipped to deal with diversity. Early in its history the dangers to unity in religious differences were recognized. Consequently our fathers decided to exclude sectarianism in religion from the curriculum. Thus they laid the foundations of a school system that might welcome to membership eventually the children of all the peoples of the earth. In the course of the years we have learned that religious instruction is not necessary for the weaving of the essential bonds of unity between these diverse elements. We now know that the ideals and the principles that constitute the American way of life and the characteristics of personality which all recognize as basic in a democratic society, are rooted in a common stream of life, which pervades all the religions in our midst. To make ever more explicit the promise of this common way of life, while leaving each individual free —outside the school—to expand upon it and to justify his religious faith as he will, constitutes the American way.

Let us hold to the American way by insisting that the school stick to its last!

Appendix

The more specific areas touched on in the Ethics course in the Elementary School have to do with the child's relation to his own immediate environment. There is a need to make him feel secure and adjusted to his world, to help him feel the dependability of the people around him, to make him conscious of his own tasks, and of the necessity to co-operate with those about him. The awareness of mother love, of his father, of the problem of sharing with siblings, older and younger, of taking responsibility at home—all these are relevant to his needs. Similarly in the school, the problems of adjustment to the group and to other individuals are of special concern to the Ethics teacher. The class teacher has the problem of aiding day-to-day adjustment, whereas the Ethics teacher helps to interpret events, clarify problems, and quicken and deepen and stimulate the child's ethical insight into those relations which are basic to his happiness. In order to do this effectively, the Ethics teacher seeks close contact with the teachers and the pupils. Frequent conferences with class teachers, as well as visits to the classroom, lunch table, library, locker room, and newspaper, acquaint the Ethics teacher with the problems that confront the pupils as individuals and as members of the group. A direct attempt is made to help. The story teller becomes the friend and counsellor.

In the early grades, the use of stories is an effective technique. For the most part, the stories do their own teaching, and discussion is omitted or dwelt upon very slightly. Often the story is reviewed or retold by one of the children in the following period. Discussion plays a lesser part than it does in the upper elementary grades. Indian lore, folk tales, Bible stories, Greek myths—literature which is relevant to the problems and interests of the younger child and which articulates the moral insights of men—have much to contribute to the growth and understanding of the child. Often, study units—historical and cultural—have formed the basis and background for the development of the Ethics program. Frequent conferences with class teachers, as well as visits to the class, acquaint the Ethics teacher with those problems of individuals and the group which should form the background of his own thinking in his approach to the group and, to some extent, affect the actual Ethics period. In the upper grades school experiences and historical and cultural studies of the class are the taking-off points for story, report, and discussion.

GRADE ONE

Friendliness and helpfulness are the dominant ideas of this year. An attempt is made to help the child feel at home in the world and in friendly relation with all things—earth, trees, flowers, birds, beasts, and people.

GRADE TWO

In the first half of the year in second grade, the emphasis is on friendship and on working together. In the second half of the year, the World of Nature. Many questions arise in the children's minds—some are answered in the science lesson. The teacher uses the Greek myths as fruitful material for the stimulation of thought, wonder, and the appreciation of beauty. Moreover, these myths afford in their simplicity a wealth of ethical material on obedience, hospitality, kindness, and essential values.

GRADE THREE

In the third grade the child begins to feel the conflict between the home, the demands of school, and his companions outside of school. He is growing up and feeling the first pull of the gang spirit. At home he is often still babied, and he is apt to struggle against this attitude. In this class it is the function of the teacher to help the pupil get *right* attitudes toward the school group and toward his home situation. What should his relation be to parents, brothers and sisters, grandparents, and domestic workers? What should his attitude be to classmates, teachers, principal, the staff? What should rules mean to him?

The patriarchal Bible stories and stories of other tribal groups are helpful at this period. As the child widens his interests outside the home, it is the function of the teacher to help him see his life in proper perspective. Some foundations for this were laid by the study of the Greek myths in Grade Two. Creation myths of primitive peoples, emphasizing as they do man's wonderings not only as to the beginnings of the physical world but also as to the presence in the world of good and evil, furnish excellent material for class discussion. The child sees that people are still seeking answers to those age-old questions. In the selected Bible stories he finds good and bad relations among members of the family. There is probably no more helpful story of this period than the story of Joseph and his brothers.

Special problems discussed by the Ethics teacher and the class teacher are frequently used as a point of departure; problems of truth telling, questions of obedience and of co-operation both in the home and in the school, attitudes toward the new child in the group who is "different," the "ganging up" against the unpopular child—all these are matters of special consideration in the Ethics class. Appropriate story material aids and enlivens the discussion.

At times the Ethics teacher sets aside the special Ethics curriculum in order to build upon a class interest that has arisen from some other source. The social science work and the science classes frequently inspire the Ethics work. On the other hand, a play initiated in the Ethics class involves a similar sharing on the part of the art, music, and physical education teachers. Such interdepartmental co-operation is vital to the school program.

As an example: the Ethics teacher co-operates when the group in social science studies the history of New York City. Dutch stories, Catskill lore, are used as a point of departure for the Ethics work. In some years the concentration on problems of the city—how it is fed, clothed, housed, made safe, etc.—afford a wealth of ethical implications. The roles of the milkman, the fireman, etc., the uses of materials, co-operation among the people of the city, help the child feel himself part of the larger community. Here again, myths come to our aid in the use of the story of Prometheus. Harbor life and transportation afford occasion to consider not only the depth of the channel and the signal system, but also the safety and the work conditions of those who supply the service. Similarly, the children's thought may be directed to the farmer and his relation to city life.

Or again, science and ethics may profitably combine a project. Here also the creation myths are again the springboard and lead to much interesting work both about the stars and the planets, and about evolution in animal life. In Ethics the part played by light in worship leads to much interesting thought. The ceremonies of various tribes are studied, and especially contemporary religious traditions. The importance of those who produce light and the role that light plays in our everyday life afford rich material for ethical consideration.

The Ethics class seeks further expressional outlets in school and, if possible, in home responsibilities, in contact with other social groups, in recognition of philanthropic needs, and in attempts to do something to "help." Sometimes settlement-house groups have been contacted and a helpful exchange of friendship inaugurated.

Stories Used in Grade Three

Adam and Eve	Jacob and Esau	The Prodigal Son
Cain and Abel	Hagar and Ishmael	The Good Samaritan
Abraham and Lot	Joseph and His Brothers	

In recent years the third grade has frequently concentrated in social studies on Indian Life. The following Indian stories have then been successfully used:

Stories the Iroquois Told Their Children

How the evergreens got their all-year green
How music came to the world
Why the Pleiades dance
How the Indians got corn
How the Indians learned medicine
How Eaglefeather received his name
How the Indian maiden solved her problem
How the Young Crows and Blackfeet became brothers

Good creation myths which are concerned also with right and wrong should include the Wyandot Indian story: "The First Animals and the Twin Gods."

The Three First Things: Salt, Ice, and Fire (Iceland)
The First Sunrise and Sunset (Central Australia)
The First Animals Make Man (California Indians)
The Tree with Animal Fruit (African Bushmen)

GRADE FOUR

In the fourth grade, the child's mental horizon expands. He shows an interest in maps and the globe. The focus of the social science work in this year is often the Mediterranean countries. This lends itself admirably as the basis of the year's Ethics work. Nowhere is better material for this age found than in the story of the peace-loving, home-loving, nonimperialistic Pharaoh, Akhenathon, "Child of the Sun." Akhenathon failed because he did not know how to underpin his idealism. In the light of the world today, even the fourth grade child can sense the need of a firm economic system, and the inadequacy of slave labor and tribute.

He is at the beginning of the hero-worship stage and he thrills to adventure. It is a good time to introduce the relationship of leader and of follower—the obligations and the duties of both. He has to make decisions and needs help in thinking through the process. His responsibilities are increasing.

The Greek stories of the Iliad and the Odyssey form unforgettable material for this age. The relations portrayed as taking place among the gods, among the warriors, and in their families are not only of intense interest in themselves, but link with the children's own situation at home and in school. They now share with great pride, though in minor capacities, in the management of the school, through the Council, the school paper, and service activities. They know that a leader must trust and be trusted and are ready to discuss the sailors who doubted Ulysses' honesty in the affair of the bag of winds and Ulysses' failure to take his men into his confidence. They are scornful of the goddesses who bribe Paris. They thrill to the hospitality and friendship accorded Ulysses among the Phaeacians, and Telemachus as he journeys in quest of his father. They realize the difficulty of making choices and sympathize with Agamemnon when he is forced to sacrifice Iphigenia. The incidents selected further reverence, friendliness, and obligation.

Some of the Greek stories used are:

The marriage of Peleus and Thetis
The Apple of Discord
Childhood of Ulysses and Achilles
Abduction of Helen
Attempts at escape by Ulysses and Achilles
Iphigenia in Aulis
Early books of the Iliad
Achilles and Patroclus
Death of Hector
Priam and Achilles
The Wooden Horse
Ulysses' wanderings home:

> Land of the Lotus Eaters, Cyclops, Aeolus and the bag of winds, Circe, Scylla and Charybdis, Cattle of the Sun, Calypso, The Storm, Ulysses among the Phaeacians, Visit to the Land of the Dead, Sirens, Wanderings of Telemachus, The Return of Ulysses to Ithaca, Faithful Penelope, The Swineherd, The Old Dog, The Beggar, the Nurse, Contest with the Suitors, Laertes.

For at least part of the fourth grade year the class has a special responsibility in the School Store. This makes it possible to consider some of the ethical questions which arise out of the children's experience in the day-to-day work of the store—service, manners and courtesy, functions, co-operation, purpose of the store, comparison with motivation of similar enterprises in the outside world. Early trade, piracy, raids, and outright war are part of the historic background, as are also the recent developments of elaborate co-operation and exchange—local, national, and international. Tests of a good store, rotating different kinds of work, sharing responsibility and taking responsibility, fair prices, money—these, too, are discussed. Stores of different types, stores in different settings with specific functions are also considered from the viewpoint of purpose and functions in relation to the welfare of people.

GRADE FIVE

The children of the last two years of the elementary school are capable of much more mature study and concepts.

Once again the rich experience and insight of the Bible affords material on the tribal life, the leadership, the emergence of nationhood, the struggle for unity and order, the ethics of slavery, and the relations of leaders and people. The story of how Moses rose to leadership and led his people to freedom, their struggles in the wilderness and the relation of the people before they found unity and nationhood—this often occupies a good part of the year's work.

Moses: his birth, early life, leadership, and relation to people

Samuel	The Death of Saul and Jonathan
The Request for a King	David and the Water
Saul Goes Seeking	David and Bathsheba and Nathan
Saul as King	David and Absalom
Jonathan and Saul	Solomon—Justice and Judge
David and Goliath	The Unity of the Nation
Saul and David	Qualities of the Leader
Jonathan and David	Qualities of David
The Hunting of David	Story of Ruth and Naomi and Boaz

In their class studies, a good deal of the time of the fifth grade is spent on the Middle Ages. In order to contribute to an understanding of feudal relationships, an attempt is made to explore the ideas of progress and to know and understand some of the facts of changing civilizations in historic perspective.

From the Middle Ages, the Ethics teacher draws lessons based on the manorial system, the relations of kings, lords, and knights, the training for knighthood, the powers and duties of kings, chivalry, *noblesse oblige,* the relations of slaves and serfs, craftsmen and the guilds, and the problems of loyalties. Serious consideration is given also to the use of force and the problems of war and peace in biblical and feudal times.

William the Conqueror	Robin Hood
King Arthur	The Prince and the Pauper
King John	King Lear
Magna Carta	The Atheist's Mass
The Young King	The French Revolution
The Happy Prince	The Russian Czar and Czarevitch
The Naked King	

The Crisis in England and Coronation

From living conditions in the Middle Ages to living conditions today is a simple step. It leads to the age-old questions of "Who is my neighbor?" "How does he live?" and "How shall I treat him?" There follow: discussions of public health and of housing; visits to health centers and to housing projects; visits to segregated sections of the city—Harlem, the Ghetto, Little Italy, and Chinatown. What does the city do for its people? What can we do as individuals? What can we do as a group? From one such excursion projects of action often develop.

Similarly, transition can be made from the religious emphasis of the Middle Ages to the religions found in our city today. A real appreciation for the reverences of others can be gained in this year. The children are interested in learning a little of religions not their own, and in discussion perceive the ethical strain that runs through all the religions. In this poignant time, when the strains between races and religions bring such tensions, this appreciation is invaluable.

GRADE SIX

The social studies of this last year of the elementary school concentrate on the development of America. Two main lines of study constitute the core of the Ethics classes: the people who make up the American community, and the traditions and principles which are the basis of the American dream.

The Americans:

The origins and migrations of peoples

Indian and Eskimo tribes

The story of discovery, exploration, and settlement: the *Mayflower;* the covered wagon, frontier days

Biographies of famous Americans: What made them develop to be a force in American life? What were their ideals?

The American Dream:

Among the elements which have gone into the making of American democracy have been the traditions and principles discovered by many peoples as they struggled for a better life: *lex talionis,* Ten Commandments, Hebraic social legislation, the teachings of Jesus.

So also the Magna Carta, Bill of Rights, and civil liberties. Again, the Will of Sun Yat Sen, and the Atlantic Charter. The supreme values recognized by people like Pierre and Marie Curie, George Washington Carver, Elizabeth Fry, Florence Nightingale, etc. From a study of these codes and ideals, some classes have tried to work out an expression of ideals satisfying to themselves.

Since the sixth grade carries the chief responsibility of the school newspaper, it is easy to move into consideration of the history and the freedoms and responsibilities of the press in a free country. Here there is also an opportunity to deal with the relations of the editorial staff to each other and to the readers; the problem of truth, accurate reporting, libel, bearing false witness, propaganda, and the functions of a paper. Not only are the problems of the school paper considered, but also the great newspapers of America. Peter Zenger, Jacob Riis, Lincoln Steffens, etc., are the subjects of some of the biographies which afford rich material on these questions.

In this pre-adolescent age, the problems of cliques, bullying, etc. again become virulent. Therefore these intra-school relations are again discussed and rethought. Above all, an attempt is made to bring the group into democratic relation not only with one another but with the younger children of the school. This last is greatly aided by participation in the school service projects. Older children help the little ones put on their outdoor wraps, make needed equipment such as dolls' beds for the kindergarten, and help during meals.

Furthermore, in the last year of elementary school, the increased participation of the children in self-government affords opportunity for discussion of freedom and responsibility, respect for differences, and co-operation with others in the larger community. Study of some community outside the school and the assumption of a social service project bring to the fore the problems of others and their needs.

Whichever of these many sources of experience is used by the Ethics teacher, the essential outcome should be to help the child understand and interpret his own experience and to help him draw together into some unity the variety of experiences which make up his life. This integration, this capacity to make sense out of his world, is essential as he moves into the high school community with its size and complexity and new freedom.

Index

Academies, 30 ff., 81
Act of 1663, 12
Adams, James Truslow, 43
Adams, John, 14
Adolescence and education problems, 62 ff., 66, 70, 168 ff.
Adolescent Personality, The, by Peter Blos, 185
Alland, Alexander, 179–80
Amendment I (*see* Constitution, Federal)
American Commonwealth, The, by Lord James Bryce, 9, 24
American Education Under Fire, by V. T. Thayer, 175–77
American Philosophy, The Early Schools, by Woodbridge Riley, 13
American Revolution, 11, 32, 134
American Youth Commission, 69
Andover Academy, 31
Anglicanism, 11, 15, 28
Anglican Church, 28
Anti-Catholicism, 7, 11–12, 35–38, 44
"Anti-Naturalism in Extremis," by John Dewey, 123
Anti-Semitism, 12, 35–37, 44
Arbitrator, The, 109
Art in General Education, 184
Atlantic Monthly, 82
Authoritarianism, 41, 43–44, 180

Baltimore, Lord, 11
Baptistism, 10, 19, 87
Beale, Howard K., 33, 39–40
Beard, Charles, 17, 22, 25; and Mary, 16
Becker, Carl L., 137, 139–40
Berkeley, Governor of Virginia, 139
Bible reading in public schools, 4, 5, 37 ff., 74, 87, 106, 111, 190–91
Black Legion, 44
Blair, W. Dyer, 88
Blos, Peter, 185
Bobbitt, Franklin, 57
Boston, 36–37
Bower, William Clayton, 90 ff.
Brown, Elmer E., 30
Brubacher, John S., 115, 118–19, 164, 174, 190
Bryce, Lord James, 9, 24
Buffalo, N.Y., 128

California, 132–33
Calvinism, 17
Canada, 151
"Can the Bible Return to the Classroom," by C. Moehlman, 40–41
Carolinas, the, 28
"Catholic Schools in America, The," by G. Johnson, 82
Catholicism, 21, 97, 123, 188–89; antipathy to Protestant religious instruction, 35 ff.; bias in Maine French-Canadian communities, 3–4; Colonial

restriction of, 11–12; state aid to sectarian schools, 81 ff., 145 ff. *See also* Parochial schools
Character education, 62–63, 67 ff., 163 ff.
Charity schools, 28, 33
Charters, W. W., 55, 58
Chatto, Clarence I., 187–89
Chave, Dr. Ernest J., 97
Chicago's Schools, 129
Child psychology in education, 50 ff., 64 ff., 70 ff., 166 ff., 174 ff.
Child Study Association, 171
Children's Bureau, 171
Childs, Professor John, 114–15, 190
Chipkin, Israel S., 147
Christian, Dr. Frank L., 110
Christianity, 24; claimed as the American religion, 79–80; in early academies, 32; George Washington on, 17; Thomas Jefferson on, 18; prerequisite for naturalization in Rhode Island in 1663, 12
Church and state, conflicts as cause of war, 9. *See also* Separation of church and state
Church and State in Education, by W. C. Bower, 90, 91
Church enrollment statistics and ambitions, 86 ff., 99–100, 123
Church Monthly of Riverside Church, 88
Church of England, 10, 14, 19–20, 28
Cincinnati Board of Education, 38
Citizens' School Committee of Chicago, 129–30
Civil War, 35 ff., 148
Colonial period, 9 ff.
Colonial Wars, 13
Colonies, 9 ff. *See also* Middle Colonies
Commentaries on the Court of the U.S., by Judge J. Story, 23
Commission on the Secondary School Curriculum of the Progressive Education Association, 184 ff.
Communism, 68, 73
Conference on the Scientific Spirit and the Democratic Faith, 109
Congregationalism, 10, 15, 21, 37, 150
Congress. *See* United States Congress
Connecticut, 22
Connecticut in Transition, by Richard J. Purcell, 14
Conrad, Laurence H., 184
Constitution, United States, Amendment I, provisions on religion, 11–12, 21–23, 132; Amendment XIV, provisions on religion within states, 25–26
Constitutional Convention, 21–22
Contemporary Jewish Record, 147
Crime, religion and, 109 ff.
Critical Period of American History, The, by John Fiske, 19–20
Cubberly, E. P., 28